Dear Miss B

Dear Miss B

Dominic Albanese

Poetic Justice Books
Port Saint Lucie, Florida

Published by Poetic Justice Books
Port Saint Lucie, Florida
www.poeticjusticebooks.com

ISBN: 978-1-950433-43-8 (hardcover)
       978-1-950433-44-5 (paperback)

10 9 8 7 6 5 4 3 2

to the memory of
Arlene B 11/19/38 - 11/1/15

for the daughters
Mary Elizabeth and Stacey Cara

and for the 58,208 fallen

contents

to the reader

One of the things I wish I knew was what kind of relationship my Father had with his Father. Leading me to my relationship with him and how it affected my life. Parents, teachers, peers, siblings, home, all factors in who we are or for sure who we become. All I really know bout my Grandfather is he was sullen, and violent, and had pretty serious dementia in later life. My Father was a bit of a brute too, but very intelligent if a bit rough spoken and curt. One of the reasons, I think, a few of my schoolteachers were so important to me; they were not judgmental or harsh with me.

We all have stories, history and meanings we take from both childhood and later life. I for sure do. Part of all this effort now is to try very hard to stay period involved. Knowing if I knew then what I know now etcetera etcetera. The 1950s, in Brooklyn, perhaps the most optimistic time in modern days; in my life anyway. I cannot in any way address either race class or ideas about equality and justice, given that, between coming of age and daily this or that, not any of that figured into my life in those days.

It was in 1959 when I first met Miss B. I had been skipped over 6th grade and sent to Jr High, Mark Twain Jr High on Neptune Avenue in Coney Island. She was my 7th grade English teacher. That I fell madly in love with her is not really an issue here, but I for sure did. Reaching back now, I never knew or really understood, what lure and attraction she had; I guess Mom? Sister? Wife? Not any of that was clear, then or now. In my 70s, what happened at 14 is cloudy at best. I do really remember the building, the hallways and classrooms. I cannot for the life of me recall clearly her face or demeanor, only being so sure she had such a profound effect on me; about words, about writing and about life.

Why I would choose to write to her for my whole four years in the Army is not clear either, now. I did, however. In 2016, I got a message on social media, from her daughter, telling me Miss B had died. Neither the daughter nor I knew each other. She told me that they had found a whole box of letters from me to her Mother. She asked me to send her an address and she would send them to me. They came, with a note attached from Miss B, "He was my student I recognized his raw talent and he adored me." To say looking over the stack of letters made me cry is short selling the effect they had seeing them some 50 or so years later.

For the next how many pages I can fill here, saying what was in those letters, what and who I was then, is why I am going to have this work, this memento mori as both a love letter now to her, and a passing of my generation who like me, both endured and either died or survived the 16 year long war in Vietnam.

NOVEMBER 19, 2019 PORT SAINT LUCIE

Dear Miss B

memories are made of this

Dominic Albanese

Dear Miss B

You might want to take some time here; it has been a long time since I wrote you. Fifty-three years in fact. A lot has happened since, between then and now. Coney Island Mark Twain Jr High seems like eight lifetimes ago. I have been married twice, been horrible addicted to drugs, been to prison, and been in recovery now for over thirty years.

I have read, re-read, cried and laughed equal over the forty-eight letters I wrote to you from my Army days. I do so wish you were still alive to read all this; however, both of our daughters will. My most treasured memory of you *alive*, was you telling me to write like I think, and have the fact *thinking about what you write* matters, too. With the letters your daughter sent to me is a note from you:

> *He was one of my students I recognized his raw talent and he adored me.*

I still do, as only a fourteen-year-old boy can so love his teacher, and someone who took extra time with me, and did not ever make me feel poor or dumb. As did some of my fellow students, who were cruel in that way teenage kids are. I am pleased to tell you I still do not fit any mold or type and the word normal is anathema to me.

1964 Central Highlands of Vietnam

That too is a few lifetimes ago; a line from a letter then:

this is really hard, it is not some grand adventure or some cool comic book war story, it is dirty hot scary and very dangerous

I was nineteen when I wrote that and this November, on a date we share as a birthday, I will be seventy-four. I do not know how to avoid a lot of the cliché or rote stories of the late 60s, a time in America unlike any other in its so far history. I was in San Francisco, for the Summer of Love, the years of fast motorcycles, many lovers, and some truly gifted friends who taught me things that, to this day, are how I got both sober and published.

I am going to try here not a memoir or a novel, but a mix of memories, magic, mystery, romance, anger, fear, and a set of stumbles that may lead me to find why I am as much as who I am. I can clear recall a day in your class when we read, or I read, aloud Emily Dickinson's "I am nobody." That and John Donne changed my life.

In the early days of my training, I hooked up with a

guy, also from New York but upstate, who was as odd a duck as I am, and we both, via poetry and folk songs, did not in any way fit this fiction of *Freedom's Frontiersmen.* We both had smart mouths and did thousands of push-ups for punishment; our combined humor was not part of the playbook *kill a commie for mommy* we were supposed to ascribe to.

A Lop Eyed Drop Out Dip Shit

Control and end, a bit different than with those marble cover composition notebooks, turn a page and start a new one. To me, regaining a voice of then, in the time of now, is a bit tricky. I find a letter dated 1963, saying:

> *well, I guess jumping out of airplanes is sort of like stealing cars, you know the effect is sort of the same*

When I got that stack of letters, I had no real memory of writing them, and as I started to read them, o yea, memories came flooding back. I also know that back then, toe the line meant more than stand tall information, it meant keep your ideas and thoughts to yourself.

Ha! I am trying here to understand accelerated growth rate, as it does relate to being eighteen and in a daily life-n-death place, thinking bout girls, Dr. Brown's cream soda, and knishes on the boardwalk. I kind of laugh to myself, about Miss B telling me leaving school was a bad move, but that she understood why I did. Of a class where I cannot think of too many of my buddies who went to college or were not in that strata I was ... cop? crook? priest? or tradesman, with a pretty common thing then: Jail or the Army.

Here I am some 50+ years later, either cross the

world in reality, or back in Coney Island scheming on how I could get a kiss from Marsha.

Other than my uncle and the mechanic at the station on Neptune Ave, I did not have much to do with grown-up men. Now, here I am, surrounded by forty- and older career military guys who are not about to give even a toss to my adolescent longings. Hard as it was, I had to fully buy into that mind set: *we are the good guys, they are the bad guys, and good guys always win.* I can state clear here, talking to one of the few guys bout my age, who, while not really agreeing with me, would at least listen to what I told him about empires and ruling class abuse of working-class guys. Fast as I could make a wise crack about being, yea, abused, he would come back with, "Where is a lop eyed drop out dip shit like you gonna make 1000 bucks a month and eat free?"

I would never be fast enough on the comeback to tell him, "Yea, and ten grand blood money when one of these Victor Charlie dust my broom, stack my ashes and leave me in a very quiet body bag." With no idea about why or how, at this point I did come home, and how many years would pass, till I got those letters, was I able to somehow link who I was then, with who I am now.

Fish Sauce

In a letter I tell her:

*on patrol, and it is ham n lima beans in a can or
go hungry*

That just pulled me right back to how the water with
iodine pills and metallic taste is a memory in my cells. I
would later find out how to make way better food than
C-rations. My counterpart, a Vietnamese born Chinese
guy, taught me how to make rice and fish in a plastic
bag with some chicken broth and water; ya leave it in yr
rucksack, and by 3 pm or so, it is edible. His was soaked
in Nuc Mam, this fish sauce that smelled really bad, but
funny, tasted really good.

i wonder wonder who

Honest

Now, an envelope full of letters that are my personal
history, but also a real record of the times long before
any one really knew, or cared, about how bad and how
messy this whole war was gonna get. I am striving here
for honesty, and in the eighteen months in and out of
Vietnam, I think I was in real mortal danger only about
five times. I can still be shocked by my offhand mention
to her, in a letter dated 21 March 1964:

> *o wow, the VC fired a lot of mortar rounds in
> the camp today, one of em, just missed the ammo
> bunker, that would a been a 4th of July in March I
> tell ya*

Innocence, wild-eyed, and if anyone reading this has
never been in an incoming mortar attack, you might not
really get how I could be again...off-hand...but hide the
fact I was terrified. In the movies, and in a lot of books
I have read about that war, I do not find enough what
I am calling here honesty. O yea, ya could be gruff, and
lace it all with *fuck this* every other word, but nobody
can tell me they were not scared. I sure was and that is
honest as I can be.

Taking in Some Sun

Reading over the letters, it seems a lot like I had no idea what I was doing other than what I was told to. In a funny way, I am not sure I know what I am trying to do here, other than record, and pay homage to someone who cared about me. And I must have been at least a bit comforted by writing those letters. A line in one:

> *It just baffles me, all this effort and all these weapons, and I am in a camp here, where no one has ever seen a supermarket, or a subway car*

Culture shock? I am pretty sure I had no understanding of that phrase, but often would talk to my pal Maddy about wake one of these guys up on the LA freeway, and just watch his face; thinking to myself, here I am in a village with long houses on stilts, on the side of a mountain on the other side of the world.

It was important that I was STRAC, did my commo duty really well, had all the code sheets, and could when called on, provide at least three handsets, all fully charged, and keep track of them from the team shack while the others were on patrol. Call signs, coordinates and locations, if they needed air support medivac or reinforcement. When I would go out on patrol, the senior commo man would always check my gear and an hour or so out of camp, do a commo check. "Smokey,

smokey, this is gray wolf over."

I would reply, "Gray wolf gray wolf this is smokey read you 5x5 over."

For the most part, we would patrol about a 10-mile square area, and not have much either contact or reason to call in. Important point *for the most part.* In a heat score, or jack pot we would call it, you needed to be very quick to call in, and let who was back in camp know exactly what was going on. In just talking back to camp it was not necessary to use code or worry all that much about your transmissions being monitored by either the enemy or our own NSA. There was a pretty strict protocol to follow, mostly not reveal patrol strength or issue a numerical location.

In Bong Son, we had five or so landmarks we all knew where they were and what they meant. As in, *on the beach taking in some sun* was code for at the turn of the river, near the first big hill, known as the beach. If something was gonna happen, bad, you would say, *upset that apple cart and fix those wheels.* Not a call for more troops or a fire fight yet, but a tip off the point man was acting like he was not happy with what he was seeing.

One thing to note is we did not chatter a lot at all. This is 1964, there is not a full out war yet, and we are such a small unit, maybe five Americans and fifty either Meo or Nungs, out on a three- or four-day patrol. Not saying there were not a few really major camp overruns; and in fact, when Nam Dong got overrun, the whole net was full of chatter; we were too far away to be of any assistance but heard calls for both air and ground support.

I am trying hard to keep this whole thing as it relates to the letters I sent, and I can clear recall I was very terse about saying anything that my Top Sargeant would have chewed my ass for. Not one of my letters was ever censored or anything like that. I was fully aware a few of the way-older guys on my team did not see things the way I did at all. I needed them way more than they needed me. The first month or so in country, I knew they were watching me, and make sure I measure up. After a fire fight or two, or some really good commo work, they stopped calling me peach fuzz or diapers.

Dominic Albanese

you can almost taste the hot dogs and french fries they sell

And Shop Class

Light rain falling here today; trying hard as I can to be accurate and clear bout so long ago, but have this touchstone of memory. You cannot go home again, as I been saying, fifty-some years ago and today. Boardwalk dreams, midway moves, Coney Island in the 50s; that half century mark keeps popping up.

It all began in a classroom. Miss B had me read aloud a poem, and, when I did, after class she asked me how I knew about Rilke or Williams. And I told her, "My dad has a big wall locker full of all kinds of books and I can take any I want." She then asked me about my favorite writers, and I cannot for sure say who, but I do know I mention Harold Robbins and Ed McBain.

I am not sure here where the whole back story should be, being a bit embarrassed to write how unhappy and not fit in anywhere a kid I was. I was very aware I was what you would call poor. I did not have nice clothes, or any money to spend, till I did.

Is that odd? I lusted for a blue button-down collar oxford shirt, and penny loafers. I had old Catholic school uniform shirts and Army Navy shoes. Not to get all bogged down in angst or the unreal self-conscious nature of early teen age years, but that sort of always feeling uncomfortable was a constant with me. I did not have many friends, or belong to a clique, group or gang.

Around the corner from my house, on Neptune Ave, lived Marsha Fagan, who was my age but way more mature, and she and I would talk. Of course, back then, gossip was more a subject than self-awareness or ideas bout how ya fit in or did not.

Side note here: I would run into Marsha in the late 60s in San Francisco, and we spent a day just going over the times all this took place. She did not go to Mark Twain, she went to private school, but knew a lot of the local kids who did. We musta talked ourselves hoarse that day, calling back names and events. She said she always liked me, but her parents would never've let her date or be involved with any but a Jewish boy. We had a good laugh bout that too.

School was agony for me. I cannot, to this day, do simple arithmetic, and only History or Miss B's English class interested me at all.

Wait, shop class did too. I had already built myself a bicycle with an automobile steering wheel instead of handlebars. When I found out in shop class you could learn how to weld and make sheet metal things...looking back, that was the real ticket out of school for me, and a lifelong job working on machines. Mr. Ponterari was the shop teacher. Nobody liked him, but I did. He let me come in after school and practice using tools and taught me how to both bend and form stuff. He also taught printing, but I was not interested in that.

Miss B had this way of calming me down and make me stay on subject without ever have to yell at me or make me go to detention. I bet I hold the seventh-grade record for time spent in detention. It sort of pains me here that I can remember some things she said to me but not the sound of her voice. Where I can imitate Mr. Ponterari like I was him. Drop my voice and speak really crisp and be kind of scary; why I think most kids did not like him.

Donaling

I would only learn, way later, the concept of *to thine own self be true*. Not to belabor a point, the hardest thing about writing this is trying to stay true to what I did not know then but do know now. This is not a war story; this is not a weepy memoir. It is a relationship story about how one teacher, at a critical time in my life, was there and did for me what so far, I think, had not been done for or to me.

Now, I can recall the building, the park alongside, and the bay behind it. Clear as if 1958 was last week. I had been expelled from Catholic School in the fifth grade, for both being insolent and telling the nuns they were, and I said this, "Full of shit, and dumb as dirt."

I did get saved by my dad, even if some side way I knew he was keeping up appearances, more than really mad at me. This is where Miss B really comes into play. On 33rd Street was PS 188, and my dad went there to enroll me. It was late in the school year, and I was not with him when he went. When he came home he told me they were going to skip me to seventh grade, and in September I would go to Mark Twain Jr High.

I got almost a full month of extra summer that year, and went to the gas station on Neptune Ave, H+L Sunoco Service-n-Repair. My first real for pay job was to clean out the rowboats and gas up boats that came to the dock.

I also got to come in the repair shop and would work on my bicycle; and I did build a minibike with a 5-hp motor, but Uncle Geno would not let me ride it on the street. All in all, I do recall that was about the most perfect summer of my life. I even got to drive cars - I was just about as big then as I am now; I got a big growth spurt at twelve - but only on the parking lot and in and out the repair stalls.

I also would get up early with my brother Tommy. He would go tend to the trot lines he had put out on the jetty the night before. I would work my sand rake, all over the beach up and down, and find coins and, one time, a really expensive diamond ring. My dad went to work the night I found that ring and told Big Wilson bout it, and Big mentions on the radio that that morning someone had found a really nice ring in Coney Island and to call him. They did, then Big called my house and my dad called the people. There was no question the ring was theirs; they knew the initials in the band. He told em where we were; they came out, and I remember the car, it was a big new caddy, the lady gave me fifty-bucks and was crying she was so glad, it tum out it was her husband's mother's ring that he gave her for an engagement ring. I was stunned. They left, and my dad gave me ten bucks out of it, a princely sum then. I went and bought a mask and fins to go snorkel with.

Some mornings I could make five- or ten-bucks...and I kept all that change in a box; I was gonna save up and get a motorcycle with that money. My brother made way more than me; he would get pogies bass perch and black fish, had a board and hose set up under the board walk, and would filet out the fish. He was amazing and had a terrible speech impediment, but he could do college level math at ten-years old. He would go up and down the houses on Surf Ave, up and down from 29th to 37th Street and sell those fish. There were times he would make twenty- or thirty-bucks a day, and he would always give Pop half or more. I think that was why he was Pop's favorite and always was.

One day, he fell down a flight of concrete stairs into a yellow jackets' nest, got stung a bunch of times, puff up like the Michelin rubber man. Dad took him to Coney Island Hospital; they gave him I assume some antihistamine or something.

This is not an exaggeration, he said in a full clear voice, "Jesus I got my ass bit up good," and I was there; both Pop and I were.

"Wait, say that again," and he did. To the day he died, he would have a few words he did not pronounce correctly, but his speech improved 99%. Up till then I was, it seemed, the only one who understood him... he called me *Donaling*. And he spoke in what sounded like gibberish. Lo an woe to anyone who called him a dummy. He was quick to fight, and was, I remember, in a 600 school for special needs kids. He like me, would leave school at under sixteen, the legal age to quit, but he was already a big-time carnival hustler at fourteen and made, again I am not exaggerating here, more than my dad made with his full-time job.

I told Miss B all about him that first couple weeks of school; it was the first story I turn in to her, about him and the stairs and the bees. She had me read that story to the class, and it made me feel, for the first time in my life, valuable and special. I cannot say if that is how I felt then but recall it now. I know it was the beginning of my love of writing and words.

Take that to mean, no matter how many turns my life took after, I have read at least two books a week since those days sixty-some years ago. I question again, what was the real draw to her? Why, no matter how hard I try, I cannot say for sure; even today I cannot. In all honesty, until her daughter reached out to me and told me about the letters, it was not a big part of my memory, but I did sometimes say to myself, *If Miss B could only see me now.*

Taking Things Apart

One of, if not the most, treasured remembrance is Miss B taking me to Lincoln High to meet Abe Lass, the principal, and get me to take the GED high school test so I would go in the Army with at least that, to not just be stamped cannon fodder.

The first car I ever took apart belonged to Roy Yellen, a bagel baker who lived next door to us on 33rd Street. It was a Rambler with a push button transmission; I had to know how that worked. So I took the dash panel off and found out it was just a cable much like a shift lever was for any other automatic transmission. He came out and was first mad but saw I did not damage anything and had the panel right back as it was. He was the first one to teach me Yiddish, "You goy goniff I thought you were try to steal my car."

I was twelve, not ready to drive, but almost all my life I have taken things apart and tried to figure out how they work. My cousin had a small gas-powered airplane with a hand control that made it fly in a circle. I took that motor apart and cleaned it up inside with, of all things, lighter fuel. It ran better after I did that.

My Aunt Irene, she was my godmother, used to bring me plastic model planes and boats. I would put them together but not glue em so I could take em back apart; I think she was very fond of me.

Wait Till Your Father Gets Home

This whole idea of going back to my childhood and make a story about it, has me up from the desk sometimes and walk a bit to be sure I am telling it like it was and not how I wished it was. I am not gonna spend a lot of time about my mother, a part I am sure of why I was so drawn to and taken with Miss B.

Mom was by all accounts a very smart and attractive woman, but she was a hopeless late stage alcoholic by the time I was ten or so. To this day the smell of ash trays or beer make me very uncomfortable and I am sure have some cellular memory of her attached. She did humiliate me, always complain about something or other, all the time. "You wait till your father gets home." O, I heard that a thousand times.

Here is a funny. I had mentioned that Tommy was Pop's favorite, right? Well one thing Tommy would do, if either of us was in a jackpot or heat score, he would run down the jetty and catch a few eels, bring em home alive, put em in the kitchen sink in water, and when Pop come home, had we done anything short of burn the house down, he let it go; he loved to skin and cook eels. He grew up on the Connecticut River, and eels were one of his and, I hear, his dad's favorite foods.

Another thing about my mom's family, they were

real bigots. Two toilet Irish, with the sort of Archie Bunker mindset that class is all but famous for. Her father owned a saloon in Merrick Long Island, called the Meroke Tavern, and he was a big IRA guy. His brother, Dennis Joseph Metcalf, is a famous WWI hero. Mom had five sisters, two of whom were ordained nuns, one cloistered, one Little Sisters of the Poor. That would be my Aunt Florence. When she would come to play cards with my mom and two other of her sisters, before she left, my dad would go downstairs and get her three small bottles of Christian Brothers Brandy. I would hear them clink in the sleeve of her habit going down the stairs.

On my dad's side, only Aunt Celia lived in New York, with her two daughters, Geraldine and Rose Louise, who were really big girls and used to pinch my cheeks and hug me. I lived with them when I was three- and four-years old while I got eye operations in Manhattan. They lived on West 47th Street between 8th and 9th Avenues, across from the original Heils Kitchen, how Hell's Kitchen got its name. It was, when I lived there, an Italian deli, and I remember Mrs. Caspadora who would watch ya like a hawk so ya did not steal the penny candy. I do remember the smell of that place and sometimes Rose Louise would give me a nickel and all three of us would share the candy. I think I recall it was nougat and three colors, like spumoni.

When I was living with Aunt Celia, my dad would come get me sometimes and take me to work with him. I got to sleep under his desk in the RCA building. O dear that is a whole other story. This one is about Miss B, and my latter days, not my innocent childhood.

There was a guy, name Ed O'Malley, who I did not know then but would meet in the Army, and he was in love with my cousin Geraldine and when he got out they got married. Those days on West 47th Street are probably the most pleasant of my whole life's memories.

Beside the fact, Aunt Celia was a world class cook.

Her husband, my Uncle Tony, had a fake foot in a shoe; he would sometimes chase me with the shoe and I would run, I cannot remember if I was really terrified, but it was a great game.

Another odd part of this chapter is the fact my dad got a job driving one of Uncle Tony's cabs (he had four of them). I would not find out about this part of the story till years and years later. My dad called Uncle Tony from 72nd and 2nd Avenue, told him where the cab was, and from that day, my father never got in a car again. That is the truth of it; he never said a word to me or, I think, my mother. Whatever happened in that cab, none of us ever found out.

Dad had an army friend named Bob Cocco, who ran City Service, a janitorial and maintainance company, for various NYC big buildings. The Rockefeller Center had just been opened, and Bob called General Sarnoff, who funny enough my dad knew from the Army, too. It began the job my dad would have the rest of his life. He was the building nighttime superintendent for all of the buildings: the Music Hall, RCA building, and the various shops and other areas of the Center.

Parakeets vs Chihuahas

I have no memory of my last eye operation, or really of that time, other than my aunt and cousins, who were my family then. I *do* remember, when my dad came to get me and take me to Richmond Hill, where he, my mom and my two-year-old brother Tommy were living; this brings back a ton of recall.

Mrs. Helen Blazajewisky was the lady who owned the house. Her and her son Steven lived on the bottom two floors, and we lived on the top one. I do not remember fully the size or much about the apartment, not like I do Aunt Celia's. I can still see the marble stairs and wainscoting; I can smell the carpet and the food, and this is 1949 or so.

But what I do remember, Steven, the son who was maybe twelve or so, had hundreds of parakeets in the basement, all in hand-built cages, big ones his dad had built. I never found out what happened to his dad, but Steven and his mother sold birds to every pet store in NYC. They were magic and a joy to me. I learned how to clean up the bottom trays and could get a lot of the birds to sit on my finger, and some of them were, I am gonna say, brood stock, because they had them for years. A few of them were long time pets and came upstairs to their apartment and were very well-trained birds.

I am about six or seven now, and my dad bought a bungalow in Coney Island that he got his brother, my Uncle Joe, to come down from Vermont and help make it really nice. Along with a guy my dad worked with who was a master carpenter, they made two extra rooms, and that would be my touchstone home. I have vivid memories of it, the blueberries and grapes in the back yard; Mr. and Mrs. Yellen across the alley, who were very nice to me, and their dog Pepe, a black chihuahua, who hated me and I hated him.

I remember, again vivid, Greenberg's produce market, on the corner of 33rd and Mermaid. Sammy (whose son David would become famous as one of the Super Cops Called Batman and Robin; they even made a movie about him), would always let me pick and clean-up left over stuff. I would bring it home and Pop would use it to cook us all dinner before he went to work.

Remember - he never got in a car, ever. He would usually walk from 33rd down Mermaid to Stillwell Avenue and take the D train to the city. He would stop at Smith and 9th Street, the highest elevated platform on all the subway line, and have a smoke. He carried a book in one pocket, and a crossword puzzle book in the other. He was perhaps the most garrulous gregarious person alive; he would talk to anyone.

His other claim to fame was he had an encyclopedia brain about baseball. He knew everything far back as the NY Knickerbockers to the current box scores on every game played. He could tell you not only what team won every world series but the scores and number of games. He would sometimes be on the Bill Mazer show on the radio and astound Bill with his ability to recall specific plays and pitching duels, and, like I said, on the subway if you sat next to him you got an ear full. On rainy days, he would take the Mermaid Avenue bus, and all the drivers knew him and liked him. I think even some of them would ask him about games and who to bet on.

36

but they all disappear from view

Dominic Albanese

Shopping for Clothes

This is a hard part, bout who Mi Mi was. He was not my dad's brother, but we all called him Uncle Mi Mi, and he was somehow related to my dad's family, but I never found out how. I am gonna spend a few pages here on the days then, and the build up to going to Mark Twain, and meeting Miss B.

Why I mention Uncle Mi Mi was, as I would come to understand later, a *Made Man*, and his partner was this enormous fat guy called Tommy the Whale. He also was connected with two brothers who were really big time mobsters, one of em ran the Fulton Fish Market, the labor and kick back from all the sellers truckers and assorted other outlets there.

I am now about twelve and big for my age. I started to take both judo and karate with a Korean war vet name Jackie Stern, who did sort of become a good mentor to me. I did not like to fight. My brother Tommy loved to fight, and he would at the slightest provocation, just go nuts, and fight anyone.

There is a bit of ethnic here, my pals were all Italian, the other group of guys my age were Irish; J Lords were us, Shamrocks were them. We did not fight with each other (much) but did align with each other to fight with the Bishops or the Mau Mau, the black gangs. Funny there were a lot of Jewish families, but I cannot recall any of them being in what we then called bopping gangs.

I myself, had three really close black friends. Remember the song *Charlie Brown*? He was a real Coney Island guy, and his younger brother Ray was in my dojo, and we were close. His mom, Ma Brown, was famous peacekeeper and block-mother for 32nd Street and was a force to be reckoned with.

Ah teenage years, and all that good music, the new (fatal) attraction to girls, and, o how I was so embarrassed that I did not have cool clothes; in fact my first stealing was at Al Sinrod's clothes store. Pleated pants and button-down collar shirts, I got away with it like two times, but knew if I got caught my Pop would kill me.

A rather tender memory, I am on the stoop and sort of almost crying, and Tommy comes out, "What the fuck is wrong wit you now?"

I told him, "These clunky ass shoes are like being a cootie kid."

And he busts out laughing, "You gotta be kiddin me."

No; I was so acutely wanting to be one of the cool guys. Anyway, Tommy reaches in his pocket and hands me like forty bucks, and says, "Go Sinrods an get some shoes an quit yr fuckin sniveling." He always had money, and I got a pair of Stacy Adams and a pair of penny loafers.

That phase did not last long, but I was very careful with my clothes, I iron em and I kept em clean. I never wore my good stuff to hang out in. In fact, I got a pair of OshKosh B'gosh overalls and some Keds sneakers. Why all that comes back so strong, I think, is just a part of my revolving identity crises I have had most of my life.

Halfway to Dead

In looking back both before and after Miss B, it does occur to me what she did was talk to me differently than I had ever been spoken to before. She cared about what I thought and why. I remember clear a talk we had about the power of language, and why some books live long lives and some just go away.

I also really think that she saw in me a fourteen-year-old who had probably read more books than the rest of my whole Jr High class. She made me value myself; that I can say the times after, what happened to me bad, was due to not valuing myself, or just plunge headlong into my biggest failings that seemed like a good idea at the time. Going back to my youth, the hardest part is taking out the whole bag; the things I wish did not happen and the things that did, had I had more or better mentors, might not have happened. More about this part will appear in the end pages.

For now, it is about both class and social order. That whole deal about peer pressure and the times during the late 50s that were, to me anyway, some of the most hopeful times ever. I can still get goose bumps, thinking about coming round the corner of Neptune Avenue and 29th Street and seeing a 1956 Dodge Lancer in pink and gray that made me just stand there and gape. Popular Mechanics and Popular Science magazines, I gobbled em up, front to back, every issue.

It would be then I really started to hang around the gas station, and began what became a lifetime occupation of working on cars. One time, my cousin and I, during my seventh-grade years, went up to Ocean Parkway and stole an Oldsmobile 58; back then those cars had a very simple ignition switch, you could work with a thin screwdriver. We were gonna sell it to the chop shop on Cropsey Avenue. We pull up, my cousin is driving, he's bout four years older than me, and one of the guys runs over to us. "Do you have any idea whose car this is?"

"No."

"Man, you two are just halfway dead an ya do not even know it. Bring that car back, it belongs to a made guy, who will without even blink shoot the both of yas."

Lesson learned. We did bring it back. We both walked all the way home, not dare to call his dad, who had driven us there, telling him we were gonna meet a friend and listen to music.

It Makes Sense

O man, I can think of many stories like that. Like being caught by another cousin of mine, who was a cop. He got me on Surf Avenue in a stolen MGA, there I am all of just about sixteen-years old, out of school now over a year or more, and top down acting like I am some Sea Gate rich kid. That car, that cousin and my dad, were how my birth certificate was altered and I became eighteen-and-a-half over night. And 99 Whitehall Street, *raise yr right hand and repeat after me. Congratulations, you are now in the United States Army.* Bit of a jump ahead here, cause this was the last time I would ever see Miss B. She somehow (I am sure my dad told her) found out what was about to happen and got me to get a GED.

Now backwards, to how and when the first time I met her. It would be September. Fall, and the time of football and the World Series, my dad would have three radios going at the same time. I was big for my age, like I said, and I cannot remember if I was twelve or thirteen, but Mark Twain Junior High was on Neptune Avenue, and was an easy walk from home. I had been in Catholic school for five grades, and I could read and comprehend on a college level; I knew that. I could not do fifth-grade math; I could not, not then, not now all these years later.

They give ya this big deal in the Auditorium, about

welcome and sort of explain the bell system and classes. Each kid gets an orientation, and since I did not have any public-school records, they put me in the best classes. Or I think they did. They gave me social studies, English, shop and, yea, math. The first few days is even now a blur, of *man I never seen so many kids before*, and moving around the halls was like this big adventure to me. I know hardly anyone cause the guys I hung around with were all for the most part older than me; I did know two boys and one girl who lived on my block, but not well.

This is gonna seem like I am in fantasy mode, but I am not. The first day, in Miss Arlene Berkowitz' class, something happened to me that even now I cannot explain. A shout out to all the astrology folks: she and I were born on the same day, November 19th. And without taking some giant leap here of poetic license, I either fell in love or had a premonition of what was going to occur.

I also have very clear memories of shop class that was way more important to me than any academic pursuits. Metal shop, I was in little piggy heaven. There will be more here, about before going to Mark Twain, but for this page, and to me the reason for this whole story, is as simple as a look she gave me; very different from my relation so far to any other adult.

I also had terrible handwriting; I tried to imitate my dad's scrawls. One of the first things, assignment, lesson, whatever, was to write a single page on what you thought was important about learning composition, grammar and writing. I wish I had it now, cause I know I said something that lit her up. Like: *If you have read Emily Dickinson or Edna St Vincent Millay, there is no other course that is more important than learning more about language,* or some shit.

The third day in her class she asked me to stay, and wanted to know what and how much I had read. When I told her I have read from Nancy Drew to John O'Hara, she was stunned. I told her I loved Conrad and Hesse, but a lot of it I did not really understand, and I do remember even telling her some sex and other stuff sort of is really either scary or silly to me. I also remember telling her I love Tarzan and Conan and HG Wells.

I so wish I could remember what she said, but I do know she took some notes and asked me about what I thought about poetry, and I told her, "It makes sense. You do not have to wade through a hundred pages to get to be moved," and I told her some of it makes me cry but she better never tell anyone that.

How can I explain? For the first time, ever, I felt like someone gets me and will teach me what parts of my scatter-shot reading are better for me than others. If only she were here now so I could ask her did I affect her as much as she did me?

Torpedos

Coney Island in those years was four different worlds. The locals, the tourists, the summer and winter time. Any enterprising young guy big enough to pass for fifteen could find all kinds of work. Cabana boy in Sea Gate, balloon boy on the midway, chairs and umbrella rental and set up on the beach. My brother, Tommy, was already a standout carney guy, it would come later he would master pin joints and skillo and other impossible to win games. Back then we worked with Looch and Joe Bronzo in balloon darts or water pistol races. Had a patter and line of bullshit a mile long.

In the winter it was lean, but you could get a job lugging cargo at the Fulton Fish Market, or, as I did, help out at the deli or the market. It is where my dad used to feed us from, with a weekly tab that Mr. Kaplan would not let us charge on, but if we were hungry he would give us food. I got to be a connoisseur of knishes and good Jewish rye bread, not the big bakery kind but the kind Mrs. Kaplan made right there. She would let me clean up, sweep up, and load up bags of flour and all kinds of just shape up work. She, unlike her husband, was very kind, and often would give both me and Tommy pastry and bagels. Their son went to Israel to a kibbutz and, while not part of my story, he had some amazing ones of his own. He and another kid named

David Bowen got picked on a lot; when they came back from Israel, they got picked on no more.

O the music: Little Anthony, Dion, just the times of Alan Freed and Murray the K, do wop, and, o man, Roy Orbison, *Only the Lonely*. I went out to Levittown about this time and asked my cousin Bernadette to teach me how to dance. She was I think my age, or a bit older, but very mature and very nice to me. Johnny Mathis, *The Twelfth of Never* and *Chances Are*. She told me if I step on any girl's feet like I did hers they were never gonna let me kiss em. I think I had a crush on her, but not like the one I had on my cousin Mary in New Hampshire I did not get to see that much.

Funny how it comes back, the Long Island Rail Road, and feeling like such a grown up that I could take the subway to Jamaica, catch the train, and have my Uncle George pick me up, I think in Bellmore. That whole side of my mother's family was, back then, more easy to deal with. Because, except for my Aunt Celia, all my dad's family lived in Vermont or New Hampshire. My other aunts and uncles, my mother's side, lived in Astoria or Jamaica.

I am pretty sure at this point my mother's dad was gone; they had a big house in Merrick where the whole family would sometimes have big events, or like that. My memory of that is not a fond one cause they all drank a lot, except my Aunt Evelyn and Uncle Hugh, who did not drink at all.

Each of these memories is a trap door, a coal chute, a roller coaster, that opens, slides, makes twist and tum that either speed of them or number of them make more. The late 50s poodle sweaters beehive hairdo torpedo bras, that whole nocturnal emission thing happens to thirteen- fourteen-year-old boys.

I will not say her name, but one of my friends' older sisters, who was I think about nineteen, took me aside one time to tell me she was going to *pop my cherry*. I was at that time totally smitten with a girl my age, Rebecca Gorman, from Sea Gate, and we would kiss and dry hump, but neither of us even knew how to go all the way. Well it did come to pass that older girl did have her way with me, and a few of my friends, too. I never said to any one anything about it and when some of the guys did say, "Yea I fucked her," it made me embarrassed and a bit ashamed. I know that is how I felt then, even if I cannot explain it now in latter day understanding. I was, I am, and I hope always to be a romantic, but sure not a knight, or a prude either.

O man, leading up to, and I can say without a doubt, I never had a sexual fantasy or even a bit of that kind of feeling about Miss B. No, and again, writing here about then, it is something I now fully get, but did not then. I am almost sure the feelings and depth of what I had about her was either sister, mother, or tied up with my then still wrap-up in Catholic myth about the holy Virgin Mary. My Mother's name, by the way, was Mary. This all comes again back to flood of memory and place.

Carol King used to drive to Coney Island about this time to take Little Eva uptown to record. *Locomotion* and *Mashed Potato*. I knew Little Eva growing up, blocks from each other. The other thing was groups of both black and white guys on corners under streetlamps, singing; I'll bet to this day some of those songs and singers were as good as or better than a lot of them who did get record deals.

This is also the time of payola; and Mitch Margo and the Tokens, local kids who hit it so big with *The Lion Sleeps Tonight* and *The Sloop John B*, they had to leave school and go to private school; well some of em did.

Jackie Wilson, outside the Mermaid Arms, on 32nd Street, was shot at by a jealously enraged girlfriend of his.

There were also tales of the Mob and almost daily pictures in the NY News of a body on the sidewalk or in the trunk of a car. A few of the guys I hung around with, those days, would indeed become full on gangsters. There were things that went on, I sort of knew about, but my dad had to be one of the most honest guys alive, he never took a nickel from anyone, and really was very stern about law and order. He did not approve of Uncle Mi Mi at all, though to this day I do not know the family relation there.

I think my first real regular job was working for Joe Bronzo in his tailor shop as a presser. Big old green Hoffman Press, steam. I got a dime a pair of pants, a dime for a regular skirt, a quarter for a pleated one, and a dollar for a set of drapes. Three days a week after school I went there, and in a week I would run through all the clothes come back from the dry cleaner plant, in one four-hour shift. Joe kept some of my money. A bit of a cry here, he told me he was saving it for my education; and he also would give me clothes.

It all came to an end when some of his son Ralph's shirts were stolen; I was blamed but I did not take those shirts. My dad went to see Joe and they almost came to blows, it was one of the worst days I can recall because my dad did believe I did not take them, and my room then that I shared with my brother was so small where the hell was I gonna hide em anyway. It would come about a week later, they caught this kid from Surf Avenue in the lobby of the building where both the Bronzo family lived and the tailor shop was downstairs, the mook had on one of Ralph's shirts. Ralph came and found me at Larry and Vinnie's Pizza on the boardwalk.

He handed me fifty-five dollars, said that was from his dad, and they all felt really bad about the whole thing.

I did not have to do with them further, but Gilda, the sister, was someone in my class with Miss B, and she was always nice to me. This is another one of those odd connect moments: Gilda was crazy about my brother Tommy. The two of them were some kind of math geniuses and I never found out if they were, you know doing it, but they sure spent a lot of time together.

when the moon hits your eye

God Bless Calculators

O boy this is another one. Way back in Catholic school, my dad had to come to the school, because Sister Francis Imelda took me to the Mother Superior office, over the fact that my classwork in math was so bad it was kind of funny, but my homework was perfect. Yup, my brother Tommy did my homework for candy bars, I might've said that already, but now I am in seventh grade in a public school and the same thing comes up.

Tommy and Gilda used to do my homework, and I got busted again, but this time I had put the work in my own hand writing and, man, I stand there telling the guidance counselor and the principal how I can do better work at home, and my dad just hauls off and belts me, bout knock me down. The two school guys both get up, and I am terrified he is gonna belt them too, but he gives one his well-known bellows about, *bad enough ya busted now ya lie bout it, I oughta belt ya again.*

I was put in a remedial math class; it did not help, I could not then, and I cannot now, other than measure or, as it would come, figure out range and azimuths for mortars and be able to read co-ords on topo maps. Other than that, god bless calculators.

Gene Kelly's Carburetors

O man, this makes me squirm, I used to get books out of my dad's wall locker, like say *Butterfield 8*, and skim looking for the sex stuff. I am jumping ahead here, about when Miss B and I would after class have our little talks and she, I can clear recall, asked me how all that reading, and indeed reading way over my head, affected me. I can see me now red like a tomato, and I will here say she knew me so well and could see I was not comfortable, back right up, and tell me how *your whole life is a learning thing.*

O how I treasured those talks. I even remember we use to walk outside along the Graves End Bay side of Mark Twain, and she would tell me about Chaucer and others; she loved it that I could do the whole *Kublai Khan* word for word, in persona dramatis.

Again jumping a bit ahead, my whole reason for staying in school was to get to go to the NYC High School of Performing Arts. It would come to pass that I was not accepted - even after I gave an audition that they (the teachers) clapped for. It was some double talk about my family and the fact I did not have the academic record needed to attend that school. The nail in the coffin of me ever wanting to go to school again. You had to apply before the eighth grade to be put on the list. Robert De Niro would have been one of my classmates if I had gotten in.

The lure of money had me already. I could make in the gas station, in a day, thirty- or forty-bucks. I had boundless energy. I could run up and down that ramp to the boat dock, scurry around the pump and do four boats faster than anybody ever could. Another mentor here was a black man with the unlikely name of Gene Kelly, who was the mechanic, and really took time with me, teaching me about carburetors, brakes and cooling systems. By fifteen, I was able to pull a motor, take it apart and do all but the machine work and get it running again, especially with Gene overseeing me.

A very sweet time, but long before this, would be the full seventh grade with Miss B, Mr. Kudish and Miss Remace; all big-time sort of teachers who, back then with smaller classes, would take the time to see if you were someone who needed some guidance.

Ruler Discipline

Miss B was a giant in my young life in so many ways; how it must have come for me to write to her all the years I was in the Army. Those letters now sit here, staring back at me, a living history of my 55-years-ago life.

Another thing that is a bit overwhelming in all this is trying to split what really happened and when, as the memories tangle up. I might even here go back like three grades to the last years of Catholic school, how much I hated it. And if anyone thinks being taught by Dominican nuns and yr name is Dominic, I gotta say it was mostly torture. Sister Jouges Marie in the fourth-grade was really like one of those nuns outta the *Bells of St Mary's*; very pretty, but she had a mean streak a hundred miles long.

Rote catechism (the Baltimore, I believe): "Who made me? God made me. Why did God make me? So I could know, love and serve God now and in the next world." Utter and total propaganda. And I was aware of that. Dare I ever say anything like that to my mother, or her sister Florence, who was a nun also?

I seem to remember there was some deal made; since Aunt Flo was a nun, we got a big discount on the tuition. Brown corduroy pants, tan cotton shirts with a green tie.

The girls wore plaid jumpers with the same tan cotton blouse. We were kept apart, boys on one side girls on the other.

My first real infatuation, Pamela Pierce, again fourth grade; in my notebook, I would put little hearts with arrows and DA+PP and would sit there dreaming the joint caught fire and I saved her. I also had comic books, hidden in my math and my religious studies books.

We had to go to church in the mornings and listen to the sermon, and I would just zone out. I never bought the line, but I was captivated by the crucifix and the statues, especially St Teresa Avila and Mother Mary. I never really prayed, I just mumble, and ya got all kinds of atta boys if you would serve on the altar. I aced the Latin right off, *adum que latificat u ven tutu meum.* Father Daily wanted me to consider the priesthood. Brother Justin would always give me an arm pinch or a pretty hard slap on my ass whenever he thought I was doggin it. And I dodged it a lot.

Come the fifth grade, a lay teacher, Mrs. Adams, who was very stern and had no time for anything but sit still pay attention and obey her. O man, more torture, she grabbed my notebook and read it out loud about DA+PP and I think I wanted to die. I got taken to Sister Jean's office and she called in Brother Justin, and they were gonna call my dad, but instead, just moved me to another class. Sister Christine Marie, known as the old battle ax, who was built like a tank and had really bad breath, and was well known for her ruler discipline.

Most of that year is a blur, all bullshit. I was quiet and kept myself entertained with my comic books and never paid any attention to any of the stuff she went on and on about. The day of the uproar, she is going on about, "Only if you know Jesus and are baptized Catholic can you go to heaven."

That was my o shit moment. "Are you telling me that if yr a pygmy and live in Africa and you hunt giant animals to feed yr family that pygmy cannot go to heaven cause he isn't Catholic?"

I could see her start to steam, and I must have made another wise crack cause here she comes, ruler at port arms, and I get up and I tell her, "You will never hit me again. I will pick up this chair and I will hit you with it and I don't care if I kill ya."

O man, the whole class is dead silent. She leaves the room and puts one of the girls up front. Here comes Brother Justin and I tell him, too, you are not gonna touch me or hit me; I am not scared of you, and just take me to Mother Superior and let's get this over with. Well we did. He tried to grab my arm leaving the classroom and I slip down and kicked him really hard in the shin with my Army Navy shoe.

O man, I am at this point sure I am going to jail or to 600 school or worse. Funny enough, Sister Jean Roseair is not at all upset, like she was waiting for something like this to happen. I already had the math homework bust, and I am sure Mrs. Adams had told her about my mooning over Pamela; who knows what else those penguins had me on. It is like 11 am, and my dad is home sleeping, he worked nights, but they call him up anyway, and he comes in, a bit bleary eyed, but not to me all that upset.

They give him the story; he wants to know what set me off. Sister Jean starts in about my bad deportment and regular wise-ass attitude. He is not buying it; he wants to know what happened. They go get Sister Christine, and she right away starts to babble about how I am a heretic and probably need an exorcism and disrupt the whole class with my evil lies. So Pop, being Pop, wants to know, "What lie?" and here it comes, the dogma of only baptized Catholics and the need to obey Holy Mother Church and the Holy Father, and sending me to St Joseph Jesuit would be my only *salvation*. At that Pop has had enough.

"Did he hit anyone?" and Brother Justin does not say anything about me kicking him. "Come on, Dom, we are going home." By this time I am in tears, either scared he is gonna go ballistic on me, or just drained cause I wanted out of that school worse than I could even say. In one of the clearest and tender moments, we are on the steps going down, and he puts his hand on my shoulder, and says, "Let me talk to your Mother bout this, you do not say anything bout the Church or any of that, I gonna make it bout yr grades."

I was mostly afraid of him. He was very quick with his hands, and I cannot ever remember him being really affectionate, but he did love me, I know that. He also was very keen on my reading and how we could talk sometimes about the news and the current events.

All that is very clear in my mind. I can smell the candles, the censer, hear the big rosary beads jangle on the habit of the nuns, and have this idea that I might indeed be going to hell. There was no one I could talk to about that except Tommy, who told in his dry way, "It is all a racket to make you be a good boy, and they all fulla shit anyhow." The end of my parochial education.

I wish here I could remember that summer and the events just after all this happened other than start to work at the gas station. I do know my mother was very upset, but, Pop, like he said, never uttered the word heretic.

I did have another brother, Bobby, who by this point is

about three years old, and my mother had her hands full with him. He was (I know now) a fetal alcohol syndrome kid. Colic, all kinds of temper tantrums, and I just ignored him. Tommy however was always very caring and gentle with him. He is not part of this story, much at all, cause by the time I left for the Army, he was five or six at most.

Test Pattern

What or not any of this matters, it is part of how I came to have some pretty hard days; how much of it is class, how much is social standings, or just any kid's life those days, leading up to the war in Asia that would swallow so many of us up and spit us out like old tired rags. Not for here. I could not have known what was to befall this country after this story timeline ends in 1966.

There was a major event that summer, come back to me now. Two guys in my judo dojo who lived in Sea Gate, Johnny Pero and Alan Rose, both thirteen like me, told me about this other judo teacher in Sea Gate who gave free classes three afternoons a week. His name was Phil Stein, and they were going to go that week did I want to come? I was ahead of them in the rank, I was I think then a yellow belt, and I was pretty damn good at judo, but had not really got far with karate yet.

So we go, really nice three-story house on Cypress Avenue, the whole basement is a full mat dojo, with all kinds of really good equipment and it was way cooler down there than at Paja Dojo, where we went with Jackie Stern. So, hip throws, leg sweeps, and a very odd kind of mat work where Phil would pin you and hold the opposite side of your Gi, and all you can call it is dry hump ya. He never touch yr weenie or anything like that. But Johnny was really mad, and we all get dressed and he went and got his dad.

We all went to Jackie's house and Johnny tells him about it. Jackie has me and Alan show him. And we do. He told us to go outside, and you could hear Mr. Pero and him really loud and very mad. The next day, Mr. Pero and Iggy, a body builder guy, and whoever the other guy was, he was for sure a mob guy in a suit wit a tie. We were told to scram, but we went in the back yard cross the street - no way we were gonna miss this. Phil comes home, he was a science teacher at some college, and was a real black belt judo guy for real. Mr. Pero starts to talk to him, and we could not hear, but you could tell Mr. Pero was give him some shit. Iggy just, I think, was there for back up. Phil starts to get all huffy and the mob guy, we could see him but not hear him, gets right up to Phil, and I am not gonna say he pulled out a gun, but all three of us think he did. The very next day, was a moving van, big as any you ever saw, and Phil Stein vanished.

We told Jackie what had happened, and he told us to not say anything about it to nobody. I think that was the only time in my whole life there was that kind of creepy sex stuff we would later learn about, but never said much even to each other.

I have no idea why that popped up. I know I was trying to remember the summer and leading up to going to Jr High. Safe to say, most everybody in Sea Gate was well off; in fact, some of them were really rich, why getting a cabana boy job was a plum no one passed up. They preferred older guys like sixteen and up, cause there was drinking, and o man, I can recall some tales of peeking in the cabana tents and seeing naked women.

One of the older brothers of my buddy was a lifeguard there, and his exploits were like Casanova or Don Juan stuff, how teenage stories and the myths of some get going. All in all it was a way more easy and innocent time, the networks would sign off, and the test pattern was telling ya you stayed up too late.

there is madness in the summer moon above

Propaganda

In the course of all this, I am sure I will come back to my time in Mark Twain with Miss B. Here is a letter, from just after basic training, in radio operator school:

This is very hard, only that I have a quick mind, can I get some of this code, and there are more rules here, than there were in religion. The one NCO, in charge, has told me a couple of times now, I need to request an interview with Special Forces, they are really after commo men. I have no idea, bout any of that, I just want to pass this course, and get my MOS, and then, who knows.

Signed "your favorite underachiever," it was.

It would come to September, and the first day of school. I must be clear, I do not have a lot of real, daily, weekly, or monthly, memories of that year. I hated school, deep, and almost to the point of I would do anything to avoid even paying attention. Only shop and Miss B's class were even at least okay with me. I was interested in history, mostly bout the history of war. With no idea that soon I would be in one, well a few years later anyhow.

One thing was very clear to me, my dad was not gonna put up with no behavior problems at all. Keeping in correct timeline here, there is no way I could know then how my personal disorder was part of all this. Not so much an authority complex, but a I am going to call it, a *pre-mature* idea about working and making money was way more of value than memorizing a bunch of dates, places and what even then I knew as bad political propaganda as religious was in Catholic school.

It was very interesting that my brother Tommy was without a doubt the king of truancy, to the point where the truant officer and my dad were on first name basis. Tommy would not go to school, no matter even if someone took him there; he would escape and go fishing or any of the other hustles he had going on.

Me, I went. Not that any of it stands out now. Only having those talks with both Miss B and Mr. Kudish, about the future and about either books or history. I cannot for the life me remember any of my classmates or just about any one at Mark Twain, other than the teachers I mention here. I did get, I know, out of some classes, and got two extra shop classes, and was on a fast track to go to Brooklyn Tech High and train as an auto mechanic. Almost every day, instead of going home, I went to H+L Sunoco Service station, and either work the gas pump or help out in the shop.

It was at some point either in the late eighth grade, or at the very beginning of the ninth, I left. It is not clear to me exactly when. I do how ever remember having this good talk with both my dad and Uncle Geno bout working and not going to school any more. In those days you could quit at sixteen, and I know I was not sixteen when I left.

I do remember my dad telling me he would deal with the city or the truant officer. That part is clear; the part about how they got Tommy out is not. But I do know Tommy never got past the sixth grade. At about thirteen he went off with Foley and Burk Traveling Carnival, where he was already a fully skilled midway operator. We were very different. I was mooneye and dreamy, and all about books and cars. He was all about money.

Dominic Albanese

just tell your hoodlum friends outside

Dominic Albanese

20/20 Psychology

Back to the part about not being a discipline problem. I kept myself very in check, did not argue or even make any kind of trouble. The disaster of Catholic school still with me, I know I did not get good grades, except in English and shop. C's for the most part, or if they had numbers it would have been like a 60 or so. I did, and I can really recall this, read the *Charge of the Light Brigade* in some auditorium deal and it went over big.

I also had this (I think I mentioned) real desire to go to the drama school, but that was not to happen. How funny if I had those days to do over (everybody must think this), how different I would have done it. Then, who knows what part of my home life, my own bad self-esteem and all kinds of psychology stuff would apply here.

As I said, I did not know my fellow students. I did have a very loose bunch of Coney Island boys I did hang around with at night, or for sure all summer. Most of them older than me, and a few of em already on the way to the criminal life. The part about school is vague, the parts bout stealing my first cars, the parts bout getting like 200 dollars stand out like stars in the sky.

Real Life

I talked about the Yellen family; they lived cross the alley in their own bungalow. They had a daughter named Marsha, not the Marsha I was friends with, but she was about twenty or so, when I was fifteen. I used to peek at her, through the bathroom window across from her bedroom, and saw her get undressed. I do not remember having a real crush on her, but, she was very well built enough to say. She got engaged to a guy from Sea Gate, name Eddy Gabay, whose family was very wealthy.

Eddy had a '61 MGA white sports car. It was the second car I ever stole. The first was a '56 T-bird, also white; belonged to a guy name Maddy Mora, who was mobbed up, and one my buddies, Jo Jo Cardillo, told me bring it back or man we all be in a jackpot. I did.

And as all this unfolds, it will be stealing cars that leads to me being put in the Army. Very common those days, make a man outta ya, and I think save em some money by not put ya in jail. I can almost hear this conversation I had with Miss B bout, how much I hated school, and how badly I wanted real life. O I wish I had the words, but the gist of it was, *do not be so quick to want to grow up*. I do know we talked about Salinger and Thomas Wolf; *The Web and the Rock* was then about my favorite book.

but when the night is over

Quacks Wacks and a Hard Line

Uff, this is hard, trying not to make this all about me, when it needs to be more about Miss B. Or, a real focus, on those forty-plus letters, where I did pour out my heart, fears, and almost a diary of what went on, my Army days. If there is anything I cannot stand it is some weepy memoir or o poor me pages that some movie star or somebody writes; they gag me.

I set out here, for a timeline and a factual historical story of those years, that now, some 55-years later, seem so both typical and a bit sad; when now I know things I did not then. My behavior in school was one-eighty from what went on outside of it. I do not see any reason here, to go on about some of the petty crime or just dumb ass shit I did or was involved in, both fights and stealing and just that whole thing that smacks of class and typical temper then.

JFK was in office and Camelot all that hoo ra then. I do know there were factors in the WASP vs CATHOLIC parts that my family was, if not directly but somehow involved in. Bishop Fulton J. Sheen then was a big TV guy, and of all the quacks wacks and assorted flim flam men, he to me was a good dude. I hated Francis Spellman, the New York Cardinal of then. The rumor of a bigger war, and the holdover of the red scare, were very real then, and JFK was like his dad, a real anti-commie guy.

I did pay attention to the daily paper, it was what I had to talk to my dad about in the mornings when he would come home from work, sit with the crossword puzzles and make me lunch. He was pretty hard line conservative (did they use that word then?); he was, *better dead than red*, through and through.

Fragile

In another letter from radio operator school:

I am stuck here, with this whole be a man thing, and I wish I was a kid again. I am top of my class at this point, and can send 30 word a minute, and make very few mistakes. My spelling is even worse now, I remember you telling me bout that a lot. The Army Phonetics really help, Alpha to Zulu, and I know em all, in code sometime all you have to do is send, the letter, as in Hotel Alpha November India. That means Have all needed information. The other thing is the Army, is a bit more easy than school, cause everything is gear to the lowest common denominator, they know there are some dumb guys here. In fact out of this class of bout 40 16 of em already washed out. If this is done next week, it is off to jump school and then, again, they tell you over and over, what we need is way more important than what you want or think you need

signed *as ever Dominic.*

The early letters are very fragile, and I cannot even imagine what I was thinking, when I sent her a typewritten copy of Lord Bryon's *Tho the Day of My Destiny's Over*, but in that same letter is mention of going off post to the library. It hit me just now, how (and I mean here and now) how her and I alone on the back steps of Mark Twain, talking about poetry and the meaning of it.

The letter also says, "hope you have a good time in Nantucket, anything to be near the ocean." This must have been near the end of the school year, cause there is a about a three-month gap, after; I must have only written her during the school year. I did not date the letters on top, like ya supposed to, but I have the dated post marks. So by June of '63 I must already be in training group, or on my way to language school in California.

Wet but Safe

There is a gap between '63 and '64, about five months or so. The next letters are from Okinawa and Vietnam, but none from Laos, another few months gap. The most regular, and it seems weekly, ones were between March of '64 and April of '65 again with a three-month gap in the summer. The summer in Coney Island, is the "winter" in Vietnam. I do see one, which must have sat there till school started again:

> *You think you seen rain; you have never seen rain till you been in a monsoon. I remember asking why the long houses were on stilts and was told you will find out, and I have. It rains so hard, and so steady, you cannot walk downhill wit out fall on yr ass good for us, we are stay in camp, but you get so wet, and prune up, till ya just used to it. It is hot too, so it does dry out fast. I wish I had known more bout Asia, all the way around, but, I am finding out, how wide and strange the world really is.*

> signed *wet but safe*

O man, all those letters, who was I then, because I do say a few times how all I can do is really act like I am okay cause I sure do not feel like I am. I am determined here not to make this some war story or daring do adventure. I am also very touched with how many times I told her how scared and how dangerous all this is.

I never once in any letter brag about being some hard ass, bad guy, or anything like that. I also think, so far I have not found one, really bloody tale, or brutal thing, not like the poems I would later write. I did tell her a few times about someone I know getting killed but seemed to be matter a fact about it. I wonder deep, how if again I knew then what I know now, would I have written differently. Something I will never find out.

many a tear has to fall

Dominic Albanese

Book Covers

Take me now to that day in September, when I would enter Mark Twain Jr High School. I only wish some of my memories were more accurate. I do remember, for sure, that walk from 33rd Street to 24th down Neptune Avenue, into Kaiser Park, walking the far west side near the bay. The project buildings ended at 32nd Street, and the park was for sure the biggest open spot on that whole island. The school took up a whole block, longer than it was wide. Blurry, the parts about orientation and welcome to your future, part education part propaganda.

I do, however, have memories of my first day in Miss Berkowitz' classroom. This part is hard, because I don't know for sure if how attractive and well-spoken she was is more important than that always feeling less than that was my backpack of angst most of those days. Of course I am unable to recall lesson plans or anything about it with clarity. There was this thing about the rules of grammar and the import of proper structure and spelling, punctuation, all of that.

Is this a projection? Or did I then (as I do now) care way less bout the mechanics of it; only the magic is what I care about. I can say for sure, those first coupla days in her class had a way different effect on me than any other school experience to that point. She had this calming effect, there was no *you must* or *you will* or this or that sort of belligerence I had always felt, for sure, in Catholic school.

My dad helped me make book covers from paper bags on the kitchen table. He picked up the one about English Lit and looked it over, telling me, "pretty bare bones here boy." But, I kept those books clean and knew if I damaged them, he would have to pay for em. That was not gonna fly at all.

Breaking Records

In the afternoons, I would walk back home through Kaiser and see the older guys playing basketball or hand ball. I never was any good at any ball game of any type. I would still three days a week go to judo and karate class. Some of the eighteen-year-olds, had a different time; I knew some of them, but they were not about to talk to me in the park, that whole thing peers, and kids are just dumb. O the cruel parts of growing up.

I did not like gym class at all, but, on the wall in the gym was this board with school records; Billy Haritakis had done fifty chin-ups in 1954 and that record was still there in '59. I knew who he was, he lived in the Neptune Projects with his mom, a Greek Orthodox lady, who always wore widow's black. Billy was going to go to the 1960 Olympics as a javelin throw contestant. He used to practice on the beach and could throw that thing a full bay to bay. I am not clear on how we got to know each other, but I do remember telling him I was gonna break his chin up record, and he laughed, "Nobody ever will." I never got past fifteen.

I remember asking Miss B if she knew him, but she said no, he had graduated before she came to Mark Twain. Now it hits me like a bolt, they were the same age, about twenty-one or twenty-two then.

I still had to go to church, and I hated it. I did like Father Daily, who by the way would be part of my getting in the Army younger than I should have been. He got me involved in the CYO, and there I met Don Stuart, the boxing coach, who was friends with Jackie Stern the judo sensei. I would not, that year, box, but the next year I would.

I Wrote It Last Night

School was just a torture. I liked shop, and Miss B, and Mr. Kudish in Social Studies, but not any of the other of it at all. I feel here, part of making Miss B more real, I never ever felt uncomfortable or worried about my clothes, or any of that with her. I think I hung on every lesson, and her every word.

It jumbles now between the two years I had with her, when the poetry started and when I would read aloud, and the first time I was supposed to read some poem by, I don't know, somebody. I got up and read one of my own; I would give anything here to remember what that poem was. I am however very clear on her, "What is that and where did it come from?"

I told her, "I wrote this last night."

The room was quiet, and she said, "Bring that up here to me."

I did. She read it aloud again in front of the class. The look she gave me is with me still. I was valuable, I was talented, I was seen as other than *o you dirty little rotter* (my mother's favorite slam of me). It was that day she asked me to stay after class, and we talked pretty long, about what and why and how of that poem.

She then (I can see this) reached in her desk and handed me a copy of Emily Dickinson's poems, a small book, with a really nice leather cover. "Take this read this and we will talk about it." I left that room on air, feeling like okay, I know what I want to do now.

Eviction

Walking home that day, I find out we were getting evicted; they were gonna tear all those bungalows down and build a project on the whole block. Of course I was terrified, my mother was beside herself, and not drunk, but weepy. My Aunt Irene came over, her oldest son drove her from Merrick where they lived. When Pop woke up to get ready for work, she gave him the paper. And Mr. Yellen came over from next door, they both were mad; and Roy was gonna call his brother the lawyer and see about all this.

It was to me as if my world was ending, right there. My cousin Jack was sitting on the stoop, smoking, and I was touched, he told me not to worry, they gotta find ya a new place to live, they not gonna put ya in the projects. He must a been about nineteen then, a grown man to me. It was a comfort, but there sure was some real yelling going on in the house.

After Dem Bums

I had already read some Emily Dickinson work in one of the anthology books my dad had. I brought that book back and did not say much other than, that is how I want to write without all the extra stuff. She could tell, again why she meant so much to me, that I was not alright at all. Monday, usual doldrum aside. After class she asked me what was wrong.

This I know was the first time we went out the back door, to sit on the steps overlooking the bay. I let loose, just bawling and rack sob, and she put her hand on my back, telling me to tell her all about it. So, I did, how I was terrified we would move back to Queens or Long Island or worse back to Hell's Kitchen with Uncle Tony.

I did calm down, and not able to voice here what exactly was said, but, it did have to do with let your parents handle this. This might have been the time she went to see my dad, (I would later find out they really were close).

What wind up happen is, Sammy Greenburg, on the corner at his produce market, saw me and called me over. "Dom, tell Patsy, to come see me when he gets up."

Sammy and my dad were both rabid Red Sox fans, and they would talk baseball all the time. What a pair, Sammy, a fire plug of a guy with his yarmulke and arms like Popeye, and my dad, a bear of a guy bout a foot taller. Sammy owned a building on the corner of 32nd and Mermaid Avenue with an empty top floor apartment bigger than our bungalow. I told Pop to go see Sammy, and he got that apt for eighty bucks a month.

It was a bit run down, but here comes the rest of all this part. My dad had paid 6800 bucks for that little house. Eminent domain, and all the what Roy Yellen called em "putz goniff traif shit heads" gave my dad 2200. Well we had about a month to move. So Uncle Joe came down from Vermont with a buddy of his, and that same guy who helped my dad fix up the bungalow, and they all went to clean and paint and fix up the apartment.

O man, Uncle Joe and Roy, who always brought home bagels he made that day, got to be good friends. Both of them were WW2 vets in Europe. Anyway, Uncle Joe finds out Pop still plans to pay off Beneficial for the four-some grand he owes. Uncle Joe goes berserk, yelling at my dad, that no, the city or the land grant guy who ever is responsible for that. In fact Uncle Joe and Roy go to the Beneficial office; Roy had a note with them, too. And in a few days or so, Pop gets his notice of paid in full. He would as I fully remember, have a relationship with them all his life; that little brown book of payments, he would borrow a few hundred here and there and pay twenty-five a month, I think. Sometimes, Tommy, who is at this point about thirteen or so, would go and pay off the note. Pop also as I remember would pay at least half the rent on that apartment every month.

i sit in my room looking out at the rain

Oookkaa Lok

School by now, is sort of okay; I am so failing in math it is not funny. All my other marks are good: A in Shop, A in Social, and A in English. The part about sitting outside with Miss B became a regular thing.

I am going to break down here, saying it was what I got from her you are supposed to get from your mother. Affirming consul, advise and a series of atta boys. Keeping here, what I know now and did not know then, I hated my mother, I blamed her for everything that was wrong. What she had was a terrible sickness, that, till I got it myself, I never would show her affection or anything but contempt. I think we both suffered from that part.

There is a part here of my younger life at about six or so, where she rubbed my face on the floor in beer I had knocked off the table. It is now, even this long later, too painful to really forget. I would stay out, after school, either go to the gas station or hang with my buddies in the park or up on the boardwalk. Till Pop got up and he would cook supper, and we would talk. She would be in the living room watching TV.

I can see that Formica table, the half-drawn yellow paper shade on the window, and the smells of his amazing cooking. There were a few meals called oookkaa lok ... just all the left over, cooked up with Rice-a-Roni or pasta and some of em were great some of em not so hot.

It was bonding time, this is also when Tommy was doing my math homework; that debacle would come out, like in April, towards the end of my seventh-grade year. Both Pop and Tommy could do any kind of math in their head, both of them could run a set of numbers up down or sideways and always get the right answer. I never could, and still cannot.

God's Medicine vs Junkies

O boy, this is about the same time of my first great teenage crushes. Rebecca and Marsha, the first a Sea Gate gal whose dad was a pretty famous lawyer up on Surf Avenue in the Tilliou Building. Marsha's dad was a city worker of some kind, they lived on Neptune Avenue, near 33rd Street. I think another book, to go on about how Jewish girls loved goy Coney Island boys. No sex here, only some heavy petting with Rebecca and not with Marsha at all. But, I was crazy bout em both. Marsha for the fact she got me, she really did, and was very clear with me about how phony it was to try to be a preppy when I never would be one.

There was the season nature of Coney Island, in the winter that far up from the amusements areas we had the beach and board walk to ourselves. Marsha's grandma was one of the older ladies who would sit on the boardwalk with those neck reflectors to catch the sun. God's medicine they called it. She was an escape from Germany and lost the rest of her family there. You could learn a lot from those alta kockers on the boardwalk. O man, Atlantic Baths, and you could swim in the big saltwater pool co-ed, but not into the bath parts. One more time, the mid to late 50s there were just so temperate and easy.

This also is about the time of *The Blackboard Jungle.*

Newspaper stories about juvenile delinquents, gang wars, and the famous Umbrella Man, some wack kid who stabbed some people on the subway with an umbrella. And another harsh reality, drugs, started to come in, mostly heroin, because junkies do not fight, and they steal. Trade one social problem for another. I did not, nor did any of my pals or my school life be affected by this. We did know older guys who became junkies, and everybody knew to avoid em.

Training

My first bad fight. I been at judo now a year or so; it was one of the Sea Gate guys who said something really dumb and hateful to me. I grab his shirt and threw him over my hip and bounce down with my elbow and really clock him a shot. My buddy Jo Jo pulled me off, and we ran. Harvey Kornbluth, whose father was some big shot guy.

The cops show up at my house. Pop gets up, and they wanna know what happened. I tell them, and they ask who else was there. I tell em. They go see Jo Jo, and what the deal was Harvey said I attacked him for no reason and called him a mockey kike Jew bastard. That I did not or would not have. Jo Jo tells them exactly what happened. It went away, but Pop was hot. "The fk you doing fight you want fight, I give you all the fight you can handle."

He went off to work, but I knew this was not the end of it. I told Miss B all about it. What wound up happening is, Pop and the priest get me to go to CYO boxing three times a week, and no more judo class. I had wanted to get my brown belt so bad. The gym was in the Catholic high school, and right away I could see what bits of karate I had learned was really gonna help me here.

I am going on fifteen, and the underclass is twelve-to-sixteen. Don the coach says to me, "You need to just train now, and wait till yr sixteen to compete." I got good at the speed bag and the heavy bag, and nobody wanted to spar with me. Don would put on the hand pads and I would wail on him. There was one guy there, who was sixteen, Henry Macaro, who was really good. You were not allowed to spar with older guys, and vice versa. About eight or nine years later, Henry and I would fight for money, after I got back from Vietnam.

don't sing love songs

Dominic Albanese

110

An Oak Tree

There is part here I bet any Catholic school refugee can relate to: sex is a mortal sin. I have since read a lot about both recovery from drugs and drink and from religion. Again, you would see the older kids on the boardwalk, making out, and know there was all that to either ponder or worry about. Innocence lost. Repressed lust, natural as any other part of life, but, man ya gonna burn in hell if ya play wit yr weenie.

There is also here the fact girls mature way faster than boys do, on a whole bunch of levels. O man, reading John O'Hara, or I think *Peyton Place* was big then, too. Who do you talk to about that? The only thing my father ever told me about sex is, "It is like an oak tree - it grows." I remember that fully. I do know, again that one time with Binky's sister in the back seat of their dad's car, would pop in my mind.

Pirates

I never really got all that then at all. I was consumed
with machines. I did start to skip out of school early
to go the gas station, but Uncle Geno got wise to me
quick, and some of the teachers parked their cars at his
station so he knew school did not let out early. There
is also the matter of labor law and like that; having me
working, whether he pay me or not, was not ever gonna
be something he would let cause him any heat.

One more great part of my life then, was across the
creek. Dirty Harry, a marine junk yard and scrap joint to
die for. He was a former Swiss watchmaker who drank
too much but was about the most well learned guy about
anything mechanical, ever.

I was trolling one day with a drag net to catch killies,
to sell for bait. I got snag and went over the side. In
about three feet of nasty water, there was a Johnson
Sea Horse outboard motor in the net. I hauled it up and
took it to Harry. It did not have barnacles or much on
it but slimy mud and crust. Under his watch, I laid that
motor out, on a canvas mat, and took it apart. He made
a dip tank with diesel fuel and muriatic acid. It took me
almost a month to get it all cleaned up, and Harry did
the fine work with the carburetor and motor innards.
I sanded and cleaned up the outside and got a can of
green factory paint. We put that motor in a 55-gallon

drum of fresh water, it started, and it ran fine.

One of the old rental rowboats was in really bad shape. I turned it over, and got some new boards that Harry taught me how to steam and bend, and drill them and attach them to the ribs. I hand paint that boat, name it Nelly Bly, and it was then mine. Of course when my brother Tommy found out, he and his buddy, Vinny, pretty much pirate it away from me. The two of them, took it out the bay, right into the narrows, and caught stripe bass and flounder and fluke and made money hand over fist.

Again so simple a time, the back side of Sea Gate was one of the most productive fishing spots anywhere. Vinny and his brother Bobby were both scuba divers, and they would spear fish and later both of them were Navy Seals. I did get to take the boat out sometimes, but I was not near as skilled or brave as they were; I stay in the bay and catch croaker and skates. Pop would cook em up, and all in all those are some very pleasant memories.

Figs and Morals

We started to, in Miss B's class, write short plays or little stories and read them aloud. One girl, named Barbara, was a very talented writer, and every time she read a story we would all clap. I had my heart set on going to the New York High School of Performing Arts. I did write some amazing little stories I wanted to use for my audition; the one that stands out is about my Nonna cooking gnocchi and baking her own bread. I did it just perfect and could act it out.

Miss B was so supportive (later I would find out she already knew they would not take me) and used to tell me I was a shoo-in. It was a crushing moment when even after the audition, they all clap and were thrilled, but I did not get in. It is to this day the reason I said I am done with school. Somehow I musta made it to the first week or so of the ninth grade, but never finished Jr High.

I could spend a few more pages here, in the eighth grade with Miss B, when my other classes, except shop, all went to shit. I just did not care about any of it anymore. Only her, and the books and the talks we had. By then I could drive as good as anyone, and could, I bet, be a full-time mechanic in any garage that would have me.

O dear, stealing, now is part of my life. Bad, but not break into houses or business places like some guys I knew were. Nope, cars; there was not a car built then I could not hotwire or drive away, all without damage. Most of em only took a hotwire from the coil to the battery and jump the starter solenoid off ya go. Morals, here I am tortured about sin with girls and could care a fig about grand theft auto.

Fat Tommy the Whale had a chop shop on Cropsey Avenue and would pay you for an out of town car, but not a local one; those he would pay ya for a part off one, but not a whole car. I tried to talk Harry into let me put some hulk in his yard, but he was not hearing it. Uncle Geno at the gas station got wind that some of us were indeed stealing cars, and he sat me down, told me right off he would cripple me if I brought any heat on him. I stopped, just cold turkey.

write it all down in a tear stained letter

Best Title

That last year of school is not all that clear, only that I knew I was gonna ditch it soon as I figured out how. What did captivate me was Miss B knew I was reading way past my age. She encouraged me, and turned me on to Hesse and Mann and Günter Grass and some other European writers. I then found Carson McCullers and Flannery O'Connor and fell headlong in love with both of them. I can still recite a page or two in *Reflections in a Golden Eye*. I told Miss B *The Ballad of a Sad Café* was the best title in history. We had some wonderful talks. It would come to pass, between me leaving school and getting put in the Army, she would come to the gas station both before and after school, and give me books, and check up on me. It was not till way later I found out she was weekly in touch with my dad, too.

Release

And so on to the letters. Almost four years of them; well three-and-a-half anyhow.

School – the whole process of that repetitive drone of facts dates and mostly made up agenda. It was clear to me more about how you would fit in than about how you would learn who you wanted to be. Machines took me to a way different place. O I could go on here, home, and all those horrible teen-age self-inflicted dramas.

Wonderful Language

I am in the shop, at the gas station; there is a motor on the bench. It had a spun rod bearing and a bad ridge built up on the top of the cylinder wall. Gene showed me how to use a ridge reamer, and how to hone the walls with an electric drill motor and a ball hone. I was in heaven. Once the cylinder heads came back, it was time to reassemble the motor. Ya put the block upside down, and it is clean, and the rods have been re-sized, the crankshaft's been polished and measured. Gene did that part, but I was to put in the bearings, lube em up with some light grease, and lay the crank in, then bolt down the main bearings.

Now we put it in an engine stand, and he taught me how to put the rings on; there is a very strict way to align the gaps and keep the middle oil ring, where it will not pump up, only down. With a hammer handle, you tap the piston in till the rings escape the compression tool, but you gotta be careful not to let the rod bolts scratch or mark the polished part. Then you flip it back over and install the rod bearing caps. This is a three-day affair, since I only came in from 3:00 to 6:00 or so.

I wish I could remember what kind of car it was, but I can say here this was the first motor Gene let me pretty much do on my own. I do remember he installed the cam shaft, with me helping to keep any of the cam bearings from getting knocked out as it went in the block. Timing chain and gear are next, with freeze plugs and welsh plugs install, with Permatex to keep them from slipping. Every surface now has to be flat like the timing cover and the oil pan, so the gaskets get a good seal.

Life in the garage back then was the place where I had not a care in the world other than do what I was told, learn, practice and careful attention to details.

It happened that I had to go to this remedial math class and could not go and finish up that motor. I was crushed, and I knew if I snuck out and went to the gas station, it was gonna be a major jackpot. I remember the teacher, this tall guy named Mr. Fisk, who could tell I was not the slightest interested in any of it. But he took some extra time with me, and as it happens, I passed that two-week class; close but passed.

When I did get back to the garage the car was gone, but Gene told me all I did worked well. There was a similar motor there and he took about an hour to show me how the distributor gear turns the oil pump gear and how the timing all works, based on where number-one cylinder is.

There is a wonderful language to it all. Top Dead Center, so many degrees before or after, the way the cam moves the tappets to open and close the valves. Another great phrase is Valve Overlap, where the air escapes, both valves close and the piston comes back up to compress the air and then ignite the mix of fuel and air. Magic, but sound science and it has not changed much since the invention of internal combustion.

I went and had one of my best talks with Miss B, musing over how machines and motors do not lie or have some motive other than what they were designed for. "Dominic, here is a question for you: are you afraid of people or are you just not afraid of machines?"

A deep place that, "I feel like when I am working on cars or motorcycles I am in charge, the rest of the time I just grapple with who is after what."

baby the rain must fall

Cheese and Oysters

I have had by that point maybe twenty or so of the back-step chats with her. Maternal older sibling trusted confidant or what a real teacher is supposed to do. Lift you, challenge you, have your idea poked holes in, to make it a more full and balanced approach to what is for sure gonna come up in later life. I treasured those talks, more than I ever knew then, till this effort to reclaim it all, files long deleted, in yup, later life.

I have seen things I wish I had not, done things I wish even more I had not. This time, 1960 to early '63, was, I am thinking here, the most important growth and form of who and what I would wind up being. Am I remiss because I do not have here classmate tales and dances and social events, all that I think are more about a High School life than a Jr High one.

I did not want to go home much at all. But I did really enjoy Pop's dinners and helped him clean up as he would leave for work. A both mad and funny memory is him and his stinking cheese...o man, he loved that awful stuff.

I would not find out till later how he met my mother. He was a prep chef at the hotel where she was an elevator operator. My Aunt Irene told me that story years later. I would do the dishes and clean up, Tommy would take care of Bobby, who had to be the messiest kid who ever lived. That little brat would throw stuff, pitch a fit, break stuff, and just be an all-around pain in the ass.

Was a lady I mentioned before, Ma Brown, the block mother of 32nd Street, and for some reason she loved Bobby and he loved her. She was a big woman, I bet 250 pounds, and had arms the size of a steamfitter. She would be on the stoop and Bobby would run to her and climb up on her lap, and the world was his oyster. I remember that very clear.

Taking the Time

I had some stories written about, o this is so embarrassing, stories of Ozzie and Harriet life: full fridges and lawns and store-bought bicycles. All that TV life bullshit that somehow I know I yearn for. I read one, and here is another talk on the back steps, where Miss B points out the part about store-bought bikes, and how special I was that I could build one out of scrap parts. I often rode my bike to school and to the gas station; it had an old Buick steering wheel not handlebars, and it was part Schwinn part Huffy part Dominic.

I was saving every dime I could, to go to Sears and get an Allstate, little motorcycle that was a Puch, very advanced for the time but it cost 300 bucks, a sum that would avoid me. I knew where there was one I could steal easy but Pop would not go for that at all.

O, and go back, she told me I was special, that I could already do things a lot of grown men could not. It would pass after I did leave school and was at the garage all the time, she would come by and see me, either up under or all over some car, and I was by fifteen pretty much a journeyman mechanic. There was some stuff I could not do, but Gene and Uncle Geno would show me, and I messed up a few times, even shorted out a wire harness, but nobody yell at me, just show me where I made the mistake and how to fix it.

Cars were simple then, rather crude, in fact. Till I got my hands on some European sport cars and found out how really cool all that stuff was. Not a political tale or a history of here, just a mention about how, I see now so clear, how much junk we made, over size overweight overpowered and most of them would wind up in the junk yard.

Miss B took a lot of extra time with me, I bet more than any other student she had. I never did get to the ninth grade, or if I did, only for a few weeks.

Alive

How I would write all those letters to her and how much she must have really meant to me, that I would pour out my heart, my fears, my beginning to feel like the whole war was a bust, and all I ever really wanted out of it, was me, alive.

heartbreak hotel

Camelot

More cascade of memories. I had found this shower hat that made you look bald. Just for the hell of it, in her class one time, instead of doing this drama reading I was supposed to, I put on that cap and pull off my shoe, and bang it on the desk, babble in made up Russian, *padunki rupaloudadant undeippledevosa*, in this just drop dead imitation of Khrushchev and the UN, we will bury you, yada yada.

The whole room just cracked up, I know Miss B thought it was funny, but she could not let that pass, without jam me somehow. This was during the Cuban Missile Crisis and the adults were all tied up, in fact they had a TV in the teacher break room and they were in there all the time checking up on if we were all gonna get kablooee.

I thought it all very funny, and for some crazy ass reason, I thought Khrushchev was a cool guy. I did not get in trouble, but later that day, talking to Mr. Kudish in social studies, it came up again, the real danger of us or them and a nuke war. I did not follow the news a lot, but I did keep up so I could ask my dad questions or have some talks.

The two brothers who owned the market where we got food were both holocaust survivors, with numbers on their arms. They were what you would call far right wing now. They thought and said it, JFK was weak, and they should let Curtis LeMay have his way and obliterate Cuba. In fact they thought all Commies should be killed outright. Now all this is happening, with all that Camelot hoo-rah, and Jackie being this hot babe who is like some fashion plate, or some shit.

This gotta be some time in '61 by now, and the project buildings both on Canal and 33rd Street are open, and all of a sudden Coney Island got a lot more crowded. A lot more black families, and a lot of Puerto Ricans; the guys I hung out with did not like either of them. We all sort of gravitate, to hang out at the Beth Israel Center in Sea Gate, that was about as white as Ivory Snow. I also know there were guys now smoking pot and taking pills, both upper and downer.

A side note: my brother Tommy knew there was real money to be made, so with his buddy Richie from the Mafia, they started to sell dope. I hated smoking of any kind, and saw these guys sit on the stoop and dribble after seconal or other of them red or blue pills. Not me, but we did start to drink, Mogen David, Gypsy Rose, Thunderbird. I had a terrible reaction, puke and get a massive headache, so only a few times. Also I was now boxing regular and doing road work and jump rope and shadow sparring. I wanted to be in good shape.

Uncle Geno was not about to put up with any shenanigans and he would pay me pretty good as I got better and could do jobs on my own, like water pumps, brakes, tune ups. All in all I do say, those three summers '60 to '63 were very pleasant. I also had my third new girlfriend, who was very much okay with all but intercourse. Ima spare the details, but we did carry on a bit. We would go to the movies and play hands in ya pants and like that.

Crumbs

O dear, now is the time about where we had found another chop shop who would take any car ya brought em. It was up Surf Avenue, almost to Brighton Beach. I might have some block in that file in my brain to not want to really call up all that slimy stuff we were doing.

It also was time for some real fights, not out-an-out gang war, but some pretty eight-or-so of us eight-or-so of them. No killings or like that, no zip guns or knives, but, there were some hell a good throw down stomp em and I sure got a few licks in. It did not really interest me though, I had not any of that anger or tough guy bullshit.

I saw boxing just like cars, the more you knew the better you got at it. My dad was also on my ass about my eyes, and not have them damaged. That early part of my life in and out of the hospital for eye operations I bet weighed heavy on him. But he did come, even took the night off work, my first Golden Gloves fight, that I won in the third round. You could not knock somebody out because we had head gear on, but the ref stopped it; I was pounding that poor kid, bad.

I did have this big revelation about that then: you could get hurt and hurt bad. There were some old guys hung round the other gym, not the one at the High School but the one on 19th Street, and they were punch drunk pugs. A bit of information I filed away and did talk to Don about it; I really liked being good at it, but I was pretty sure I did not have what it took to go big time. There were a few guys just a bit older than me, who even though now you could spar with each other, if you're sixteen or over, no way was I gonna get in the ring with them. I do very much credit both Father Daily and Don Stuart for keeping me from dope or booze or being rummy.

That and my final year with Miss B all sort of melds now into a maze of what was important and what was a bit painful; everybody chooses to forget those parts. Like this never being able to take anybody to my house, because Mom would by late afternoon be fully shit faced, either maudlin or belligerent, very sad state of affairs. I think, looking back, Tommy was a saint the way he made sure Bobby was okay. I ignored that kid, but like I have said, I stay out of the house as much as I could. It would pain me, deep, to go to other guys' houses and their mom had cookies and was so nice, the joint was clean, and they were very glad to be good hostess. I get sort of maudlin myself over some of that part of those years.

gone for soldiers, every one

Tap Dancing

Bout time to abandon the youth, rambunctious fan dance and frolic of those days, and go to 99 White Hall Street and take one step forward raise ya right hand and kiss momma n daddy goodbye.

First, that physical exam, cursory at best, but a lot of guys were rejected, eyesight hearing or other medical stuff. Me, they said I was fit as a fiddle. You do not get to ask questions or have any real idea of what comes next. I am going to have to be sort of general here, because I do not remember a lot of my thinking or feeling; it did seem like some grand adventure.

Being volunteer for the draft, with a US service number, is a two-year hitch. So, about fifty of us get on a bus to Fort Dix, New Jersey. I did not know any one of the guys I was with, it was mostly guys from upstate or out of town. You get off the bus, and there is like five more buses with you, from Philly, Boston, Baltimore and about 300 guys. Before you even get off, some really loud NCO get on and start yelling at ya all, *you will line up and you will do as you are told, or I will jump down your throat and tap dance on your tonsils.* Or words to that effect.

What a ragged bunch, with a few prior service guys who do know what is about to happen. They do not march you or do anything to let on. The guy who sat with me, name Ryan, was indeed prior service, and we talked a bit of the Army.

Haircut, bald just about, then they line ya up, and tell ya to strip down to yr skivvies. Shots, with this fucking gun that shoots all kind of either vaccine or I think mind control potions. Ya leave all yr clothes in a pile, and to this day I bet some NCO makes money off them. You file in this giant warehouse deal. Ya get fatigue pants n blouse (they call it a blouse), four sets of em. Ya get measure for a dress uniform but ya don't get one then. They are way more careful to measure your feet, ya get two pairs of combat boots and one pair of dress shoes.

The Green Machine

The shoes they give you are the exact same ones I been grouse moan bitch and complain of wearing my whole growing up life. Not exactly gun boat brogans, or Foot Joy. Nope, clunky ass round front army navy last shoes, then six pair of olive drab socks. Six pair of drawers cotton with elastic band, six white T-shirts. You sort of dress as you move along the line, there is a big bucket to dump your skivvies in. You come out, in a green mass the haircut the uniform and everything they can do to rid you of any unique or different look.

YOUR ASS IS IN THE GREEN MACHINE YOU WILL OBEY MY EVERY COMMAND

By now, they have broke all the 300 down to I think about forty-or-so, and you get put in a Company, name from Alpha to November. Now, they make you *dress right dress*, meaning you gotta be in line ten-or-so to a line stacked up four lines deep and equal distant to each other front back and sideways.

O shit, all the time there is this running yelling going on, about fatso or skinny or maggot or shit bird or momma's boy, anything to demean or make ya not wanna look at who is yelling and for sure not wanna open yr yap. That guy Ryan is still next to me, and tells me this is all bullshit, but has a serious purpose: anyone who starts to bawl or act stupid is gonna be put in some other company. I think to myself they gonna get put in a camp for dummies or some shit.

They now tell you to fall in order alphabetically. They have not yet printed the name tags or the dog tags, but they do just about everything anyway they can A to Z. I am put next to Dieter Albrect, some guy from Rochester a bit older than me (remember everybody there is older than me). Seems like a pretty calm and alert guy. Now they march ya, not in cadence yet and it really is sort of silly walk, because nobody is in on the way all this is gonna work out.

There is this whole line of WW2 wood barracks, and each group stands outside, loaded down with all the clothes and boots and they tell you file in two at a time, take the bunk furthest from the door till the bottom floor is full, then two more at a time go up to the second floor. Me and Dieter, get the far bunk in, but damn if it is not right next to the room where the drill sergeant sleeps.

Fall Out

Now comes that part. Lester C Edwards. A sergeant first class three stripes up two stripes down. *Mens, you ass is belong to me, I will make you all lean mean fighting machines or kill you dead.* Nobody says a word. He is about six-foot-two, rail straight and his skin is as black as any black man I had ever seen.

There is as I look back a very clear and well-set pattern to all this. Ya get a bunk a footlocker and a wall locker. There is just enough space between bunks for two wall lockers and just enough room in front for two footlockers at the foot of the bunk.

By now we are hungry (I know the fuck I sure am). Sgt Edwards calls up the stairs *fall out*, and they all come running down, then he tells us to join them outside. My first trip to the mess hall, we are not marching yet, not more than a pack of mostly bald mostly confused what the fuck have we got our self into this time. That first meal is not all regimented or anything more than you walk to the rack, get a tray and walk along the steam table; they put food on your tray. I would be fulla shit here to say I remember anything about what they served, but Ryan did tell me they put saltpeter in the potatoes to keep ya from getting boners. I know for sure I avoided any potatoes my whole fucking army life.

We go back the barracks and there is a footlocker open in the middle of the floor with a full-on demo of how your locker better look. There is a tray on top where you must put your socks folded just so down one side. I cannot remember if you get toilet stuff or if ya gotta buy it, but the other side of the tray is only for your razor and soap and it gotta be in a plastic dish, covered. You pull up the tray, and all your T-shirts and drawers cotton with elastic band go there. When your dress greens come they go in your wall locker. The top bunk boots go head of the bed bottom bunk at the foot. And there is no even thought of any deviation. *You will follow every rule or you will do pushups till you drop.*

Proud Rifles

OK, enough you get the idea. Demoralize and unify you, body mind and soul. Funny enough, on each bunk is like five envelops and ten sheets of paper, printed with PROUD RIFLES NOVEMBER COMPANY FT DIX, and they tell ya you got about an hour of personal time to write a letter home.

I do, I send my first letter to Miss B:

> *This is way worse than I thought, they are not kidding around at all, they say we gonna be killers we gonna be death to the enemy and protector to the nation, I sort of at this point wish I had listen better to you, an stayed in school and been a good boy*

February 1963.

Why her? I think, I was partly glad to be outta my family, and already a bit scared, and of all the people in my life so far, Miss B always seemed to both get me and make me feel okay.

I remember going to some classification briefing where the guys who did enlist for four years get to ask for either a duty station or MOS [military occupations specialty]. If you are a two-year draft you only get what and where they want you. No choice or even any say in any of it. But, they do give you this whole battery of tests that would later really do me good. The first week or so is only more yelling, learning how to march, learning how to do daily physical exercise, and like everything, doing it in order and formation.

There is one distinct thing Ryan, who by now is sort of my buddy, teaches me: the sharper you keep your uniform, and no matter how dirty it gets, you wash it and hang it up, and the cleaner you look the less they fuck with ya. There were some guys, I do remember, who were utter slobs; did not wash their clothes nor their nasty ass.

Maybe you heard the term *Blanket Party*. One guy stands out in my memory; his name was Beale, he was from Maine, and how he got past the psyche test or any of that is amazing. He was, to me anyway, retarded; he was always late, never tuck in, and a bit stinky. The unsaid is you can take this kind of in the barracks stuff on your self. A few guys wanted to beat up Beale and make him clean up. I was so against it and felt sorry for him, but they did any way. He just vanished the next day. I never did find out what happened to him.

Badge

The company is now in squads, and somehow I manage to get on Ryan's squad. That he is the squad leader I think was one of my biggest helps, because I was not really all that shaped up, yet.

In my second letter to Miss B on that basic training stationery:

> *I think some of these NCOs are just reincarnated nuns who have come back to torture me some more*

I meant it to sound funny, but I did sort of believe it.

Now comes rifles, M-14s gas operated semi-automatic 7.62 caliber, and I fell in love with my rifle. They make you grab your dick, hold out your rifle with the other hand and shout out, *This is my rifle this is my gun my rifle is for fighting my gun is for fun* (or some dumb shit). But now, it is all about infantry, *Every one of you swinging dicks is a grunt, you will all be basic infantry whether you go to helicopters or become a cook, you're all Proud Rifles.*

It goes on, eight weeks, and by halfway, you can march, do close order drill, and after an hour every day of PC+M (condition and motivation) we are all in good shape.

The first trip to the firing range is not all that

complicated, but it is the first time, for me any way, you get to fire a real rifle and I am just like I said, in love with it.

We are now doing forced marches with the rifle and a rucksack, singing, *Ain't no use in going home Jody got yr girl and gone, soldier soldier don't be blue Jody got yr mama, too.*

Then qualification with the rifle; I am not brag here at all, but somehow I fire twelve rounds all in the target, not one high miss or low, and tight shot groups like they told us to. The Range Safety Officer and some spotters are up in the tower, and they see who is good, who is not. I do not remember what happened if you did not qualify, but I do remember about six of us were told to come up to the tower and stand by.

Now, both my Sergeant and some other one, who is like a weapons expert or something, takes out these older M-1s with a scope on them, and tells the six of us to assume the prone position on the firing line. The M-1s load different than the M-14s; they do not have a magazine, they have his cluster of six bullets I think, and they load from the top.

We only get one practice round to feel the recoil and be a bit more familiar with the weapon. I did not need it and cannot say why, other than for so long in my life I had closed one eye any way; even though they did fix my lazy eye, my left eye has always been better than my right one. The Expert calls to the target line and tells them to raise up at whatever distances he wants. We get told to be ready to fire at three different ranges, and wind and sight line are already dialed in the rifle to the furthest we will shoot at. Three of us just nail the shit out of it.

Then they give us 45 caliber pistols and have us

stand and fire seven rounds at about twenty-five yards. I do okay but not near as good as I did with the rifles. 45s are really hard to be accurate with, but one guy nails it, he put every round in the black. He is going to sniper school sure as shit. I get my expert badge and sharpshooter medal. I am like shit this is easy. It is not.

Sgt Edwards that evening asked me how I ever learn to shoot like that, and I told him I had no idea, only that I think being a mechanic all machines like me. He would from that day, go way more easy on me, and he sent me to this other company to go back to the range with them, and I did just as well that time as the first.

I write Miss B:

I am now an expert rifle shot, and it seems they like that, I also got a chance to take some more aptitude tests I think they are gonna send me to Radio School

Lessons

I wish so bad I had the letters she wrote me, because in the next one I write her:

Yes radio operator does sound a bit more safe than 11B dogface front line grunt

There is another incident in hand to hand combat training where I tell the instructor I bet I know as much or more about this than he does. That did not go over well at all.

"O yea what you some kind of tough guy?"

Thank you Ryan, "No Sergent, I know him to be a golden gloves champ and he knows judo, too."

I was a bit scared that I pop off, but the guy gives me the fisheye, and tells me to show him. I forget the drill, but you're supposed to parry or block or somehow not get hit. I remember this well, I just wait for him to show me both what side he is strongest on and how he holds his feet, and I do not fall for his, *Okay, attack me.*

Nope, I tell him to attack me, and he makes the most classic mistake you can ever make with a judo ka: he come in high, like he is gonna grab me, and I swing low, sweep his feet out, and land on top of him pinning his arm and he tells me let him up. I do, and he is not mad or anything but has me show him some basic moves that

I know so well, they are ingrained in me.

Another just bit of only if I had known I never would let on, or even tried so hard at the range to do so well. It all will come up later when I am done with Basic and in Radio Operator training and doing really well.

'twas not so long ago

Wings

They watch ya, you belong to them, and they are always looking for talent or skill or some way to use you more to their advantage, not necessarily yours. I see here another letter to Miss B:

> *the phonetic alphabet is so easy, and the Morse code and the mechanics of communications are very similar to what I learn wire repair on cars, this is not hard, but it is very interesting. I had no idea about some of the things here like antenna masts and net control stuff, where you can hear everyone, but they can only hear you if you allow them to. Sort of like Buck Rodgers stuff to me*

I wonder what she really thought about all that, then.

I pass thru that course and am now *Intermediate Speed Operator*. This is where I really mess up, not that I knew that then, but now comes, in that part of all the tests you took, how they can use you best. Again being a two-year draftee, you do not have the option to say I wanna be in the motor pool I wanna be in this or that.

I ask about going to jump school and getting in the Airborne. I had asked Ryan about that back in basic and he said he would be going back to Airborne, but he had been out for over three years, so he had to go back to jump school.

Lo and behold, they say yes, and the next stop is Fort Benning, Georgia. Who do I meet on the bus going down? John Gallivan Madison, who will become my best friend, and from that day on we are just about inseparable for the rest of our Army days. He is a major wise guy, way more than me, smart and just movie star handsome, with some of the best stories I have ever heard about both sex and motorcycles.

Now comes this deal at Jump School, where this guy shows up with a green beret and is really like a poster man for what anybody who ever read *Two Fisted Tales* or *Sgt Rock of Easy Company* would wanna be. But the proviso is, if ya passed the test, ya gotta sign up for two more years. Not me, nope.

But both Maddy and I take the test. Three weeks of Jump School, more torture, more push-ups, running every day, and learn how to land, how to brace up, how to be a paratrooper. I do not think I am all that thrilled with it, but Maddy tells me, we gonna have fun. And I have to say we do. I think you make five jumps, or three, but after the tower and the rope drills shit, jumping is easy.

Some guys did get hurt on the tower jump, but I kept telling Maddy that my being from Coney Island and climb up the tower in the winter, musta been a sign this was gonna happen. You get your wings, and there is no way to deny now you are special. And you get to wear your combat boots with your dress uniform and this really cool glider cap, not that dumb-ass visor round thing.

I remember going home on a five-day pass, and being pretty damned puffed up about it. This is June, so school is closed, but I did go round to some of my pals and Sammy Greenberg gave me twenty bucks and told me to take a gal to dinner and a movie, he said he was proud of me.

When I got back, Maddy convinced me to take the extra time, and go to special forces training. But they balk. You were supposed to be twenty-one and at least an E-4. I was, they think, nineteen and I am an E-3, but I had done so well on the written test they said, you can go, but if you wash out, you are headed to a regular Airborne Division.

There are no letters from this time till about eighteen weeks later, and I am not gonna go on-n-on about training and all that. Suffice to say, it is more physical and mental torture, they do want to break you, and a lot of guys wash out.

Beret

Back to where I said all those tests would come in later. It turns out that I have some strange gift with language; I can already speak Italian just about fluently. So, instead of the full twenty-six weeks of training group, they send me to Fort Ord, California for language training in Vietnamese and Cantonese.

Little did I know, first letter:

O wow California is another world, you know how much I love the ocean there you should see the one here, way bigger and wider and wilder, in a room all day with headphones on I feel like a parrot they are teaching to say Polly want a cracker or hello pretty boy on n on with all the stuff ya need to understand basic zipper head talk

I did say that, I really did. By now, it is clear to me we are headed to Asia. What happens to me is I get an award for top marks, get taken to Travis Air Base to meet up with my training group class and get sent to Okinawa.

While I was in Fort Ord, I did get to go up to San Francisco a couple times and fell in love with that city. I did see this green house up on Bernal Heights back then that I would later live in and my daughter would be born while we lived there. But that is not part of all this.

Here is Maddy, "Look at you poor excuse for a trooper, and out here get sun tan, while I did all the work to keep you in group."

"Aw fuck you, I ace this language test, and when do I get my beret?"

He had his and he really looked good in it. I get mine in Okinawa, where we are now assigned to 1st SFG (Airborne) and within two weeks will be in Laos.

Asia of the Mountains, Asia of the Sea

For some reason, I suspect due to being June and July, there are no letters to Miss B from Laos. It was not any big, dangerous time, or very exciting, just mostly putting in radio telemetry devices along the hills leading to the Mekong River. That, and getting to know my teammates, all of whom were way older, way more pro-soldiers, and not much for interaction that was not about the mission.

There is also the fact that Laos is one of the most beautiful places on earth. For sure where we were, rolling hills, wide expanses of jungle, about sixty miles west of Vietnam, with the wide dark river between us.

There was a lot of CIA stuff going on. Black airplanes and helicopters with no markings, no patches, all full of state-of-the-art communications gear. There were other Special Forces teams spread out training the Royal Lao Army, and in fact engaging the Pathet Lao every chance they got. If I am not mistaken, and I do not think I am, some of the first HALO (high altitude low opening) parachute jumps outside of training group happen here.

As I recall, we were there less than three months. My main job was to communicate with both HQ in Nha Trang, and C Team HQ in Korat, Thailand. Giving coordinate locations of the *beepers*, what we called these stakes that would guide pilots over the hills in low cloud cover into the cross river hills of what then was called the Hong Teng Trail, later to be called the Ho Chi Minh Trail. The two top intel-sergeants would tell me who to call and what to say; there were not coded messages or anything but a series of numbers and locations.

It was hard going, too, because we had to carry all our food and supplies. We did have some Lao guys to help carry, but no Lao speakers. Some of them did speak and understand Vietnamese so I was able to talk to them; to be honest, I do not think they liked us very much. I would later learn they made way more money in Plum City working for the CIA.

We did get to the river, and navy swift boats, both metal ones and inflated ones, took us across. When we got to Vietnam, we went up one rather large mountain and to a big clearing on the other side. We set up a hasty perimeter and I called in to the 14th Aviation Battalion to give our location. They came with a Chinook and two HU1B gunships as escort, and we flew to 5th Special Forces HQ in Nha Trang. There were about thirty of us, and we would be broken up in teams and sent to different camps. All I could really hope was I would stay with Sgt Pratt and Maddy. Sgt Pratt was a crusty old WW2 and Korea vet who was so sharp and knew, even then, this was gonna probably turn out bad.

Sleepwalk

My first letter to her from Asia, dated Dec '63 with a return address of APO SAN FRANCISCO 9114:

We got this lecture, bout operational details locations and all like that, to not say any of that in any way to anyone. OK but safe to say I did get to spend 2 weeks on Okinawa, and I am just spellbound with the place, one of the guys here who is what they call permanent party, has a little 125cc Honda motorcycle, that he let me ride. I went from where we are staying, to one end of the island to the other, Naha to Nago. On the bottom of Nago is this perfectly round small island that used to be a leper colony, and the water, all round it is just perfect, but I hear it is full of sea snakes, and may be some other critters I do not want to tangle with. I did get to see the oldest Karate dojo here, I found out this is where Karate was begun, it is very crowded, and has lot of these little cars, that zip around like banshee banzai driver. They gave us a talk about Ryukyuan incident you cannot get in any beef with the locals, even though it seems to me they all make money from the our bases here, pretty exciting, it been a few months since I wrote, ya, and suffice to say I been on some wild walks in some wild places, and now I am in Vietnam, just where I do not think I am supposed to say

as ever Dominic.

The last few months had been pretty crazy, and I am sure it is gonna get even more crazy. I sort of had this outside idea I might get to stay here in Head Quarters; it is rather cush, we stay in tents with big fans one in one out and got real showers and real food. There is a Head Quarters company, where all the support staff and the paymaster and supply depot are.

We did all get new jungle fatigues and new jungle boots, they are sort of a green mesh on the side with hard bottom and knobby tread. We also all got issued 45 pistols, and trade our M-14s for WW2 Carbines that are lighter. It is really like an arms bazaar, they got cool old grease guns and Thompsons like Al Capone and the boys had.

They also got *Blooper*, an M-79 grenade launcher that looks like an old blunderbuss but shoots a 40mm grenade that will in fact ruin your whole day. I had never used one, but Maddy who'd been to Advanced Infantry training had, and he got three of them; he was a master conniver, and since he was cross trained as a weapons NCO he could pretty much get what he wanted.

None of us knew where we were going, or that we would be on an A B or C team. I did hear Maddy and Sgt Richards talking about mortars and recoilless rifles, and 50 caliber machine guns (gulp). The CO of 5th Group did assemble us all in front of HQ and there were some photos taken and then we got this big operations talk about both hamlet pacification and civic actions, and most all of it just went over my head.

Silly Ass Code

My second letter, Jan '64:

Christmas came and went, mostly what I liked was they ship in a real turkey dinner, and we ate off plates, and man all these guys really drink a lot, half of em were not falling down or pass out drunk, but they for sure were feeling no pain, I it summer here, and it is so hot, all that bout fry an egg on the sidewalk, on the either metal of concrete walk ways, if you do not have yr boots on, you will crisp up yr tootsies. I never felt heat and humid like this, ya sweat just sitting around, and ya gotta take salt pills and put iodine in ya canteen, it tastes terrible, so most guys just drink beer, or pop, here I am 10,000 miles away and there are coca cola machines everywhere. Somebody is rake in the dough, and ya gotta go get quarters, from the supply guy, but, (don't tell no one, I been using slugs in coke machines since I was 11) ya find em in electric out lets, and they been building so much stuff here, I got a bunch of em, but drinking soda is not help ya thirst. I got me some Pineapple juice and I did boil some water, put ice in it and drink that. All the other guys drink beer, I am not fond of beer, but it is so hot, an ice-cold dark San Miguel is really refreshing, only one, I am not about to wind up an alky, and you know why. Soon we will find out where we are going, and what I hear is they do mail call once a week, but some places do not get mail but once a month we will see

It was in January, when we, Sgt Pratt Sgt Madison Sgt Ely, and I am now a Spec 4 with eight other guys, two officers and six more NCO, are on an A-team, Detachment A-131. I think the team numbers are sequential so we would be the hundred and thirty first A team, and we got orders to go to Bong Son, or Gia Vuc, and we found out some teams get split up, six here six there.

The XO is a wild bit of work, Hugh T Harpole, a second lieutenant, who had been an NCO before and went to OCS. This you cannot make up, one of the demo guys, a Sgt Huffman, had thrown then Sgt Harpole out of training group. Then when he got his gold bar, he went back through as an officer, now he was de facto Sgt Huffman's superior officer. I sort of remember they had a talk and agree to bury any bad shit from before. Harpole was about 5'5 and built like a cinder block. He was a ranger and about as gung-ho as anyone.

The commanding officer was named Capt. Luck, who I only remember talking to a couple of times, when he wanted me to send some info to another team or to HQ. We did get split up, six of us in Bong Son, with two not Special Forces medics, and six in Gia Vuc, with a pretty big company of Nungs, Vietnamese born Chinese who were mercenaries. We got about twenty of them, and there had been a team in Bong Son since '62 training the Mountain Yards, and there is a book somewhere written by some then Captain, called Village Defense, sort of a training manual, or how to deal, with the Hmong and Meo. Only the two intel-sergeants were in on all that.

My job was to set up the commo shack, and I did have a way cool old '49 WW2 desk radio and a foot locker full of PRCs, both 13s and 14s, that had a crystal set in them so they could be used with a leg key for code or voice, with this silly ass code card where ya got words from the bible or from some state side newspaper and ya say some silly shit like Oscar night in Hollywood, and the guy with the same card would read, Camp is quiet an all is secure, or some shit.

Bamboo and Batteries

Another letter, from this time, I think before we left for camp:

Vietnam, nothing I ever read, saw or even heard about, could prepare me for this. Beside the heat and muggy, and smelly of it all, the moving walls of animals and people, the market is not like Bohack or A+P I tell ya that, they got live ducks chickens pigs, baskets full of fish, and vegetables' I have never seen, with giant fruit some of it, still on the branches. Even if I do speak, this language, there is no way I could keep up with the chatter and speed, everyone seems to be argue, bout price or quality, and they all wander in and out, there do not seem to be any men, all women, some of em with really red teeth and gums, they chew betel nut, and spit everywhere, seems to me like spitting is a sport over here. They all smoke, and some of em I know smoking Marijuana , out of clay pipes. Kids walk the ducks, it is just beyond imagine how many ducks, you see, and the traffic is so noisy motor bikes a lot of old French cars, and Quan Canh, (white mice) Vietnamese military police in jeeps, all American Jeeps. The beach is paradise, there are these palm front roof beach houses, where they sell 33 beer, and what Maddy calls tiger piss,

Beer Larue. You can order crabs or lobsters and
the kids dive in the water and bring em up alive.
There are also lots of outdoor food stalls, we call
em Howard Johnson, and you really do not know
what they are serving, but the noodle soup is so
good, and the lemon grass with this hot sauce that
will fry your eyeballs green. Mostly we only got
to go out an around a couple of times, and the HQ
is fully gated and guard by Vietnamese, who are I
hear trigger happy, there is a strict deal ya gotta
be in by dark. On the lower end of the town, I know
there are whore houses, but there is no way I am
gonna get involved in any of that, some of the guys
have gone there, and to me, nope, the VD films they
showed us got me terrified of any of that.

Then there is like a month or so lag, I am sure that
is when we went to Bong Son, and a whole other world
that. Long houses, on stilts, with deep slanted bamboo
roofs, and extremely intricate designs carved on the
doors and steps. This village I bet has been here before
Washington left England, and it is very obvious the Meo
do not like the Viets and the Viets do not like them. The
dialect is way different, and they all have either X or Y
as a first name.

The women are small and very quick, we look like
giants next to them. The medics have set up a big clinic,
and are giving all the kids shots, and some of these
people have sores and scars and I seriously doubt any
of them have ever seen a real doctor. They gave me this
guy, named Cam, who is Chinese, tall and can speak
just about any dialect up here; he is very smart, been to
college in Paris, and has this way about him I really like.
I showed him how to use the radio, and Sgt Pratt just
about tore my head off, yelling at me not to let anyone
near it till he has them all checked out.

This is about the same time of the rather famous Green Beret incident where some team found out the guy they had as a translator was a VC plant, and they took him out an shot him. It got crazy on the radio for a couple of days, and when I went back to Nha Trang on a chopper for re-supply batteries and new web gear for the radios, it was a big flap. I even saw a copy of the *Herald Tribune*, where it was on the front page. It was later to be learned that half of the camps had VC plants in them. We did find one guy with a map of the camp and Cam and Mr. Soy, the leader of the Nungs, just took him away. We figured they shot him, too.

Soldier Boy

My first patrol, up in the hills, hard to even say, how not only is it hard to pass thru the jungle, but when ya do get on the hill side, the rocks, sometime fall, and you gotta be very careful how you move, there are a lot of cracks and pretty deep holes, ya fall in one, and it is good night Irene, not to even mention some spots might have an enemy ambush and they gonna blow you to perdition.
I have two Radai guys who help me carry the battery pack and the antenna mast, but after Top yelled at me, nobody gets near the radio. So far it is more like some movie than it is a real war, but, bugs, snakes, birds who are loud, and monkeys who make more noise than you ever heard, one of the Yards told me when the birds and monkey are quiet you got a big problem I think I know what he meant, also there is this elephant grass, that is like 10 feet tall, and it is razor sharp, the point guy has some Yards with him who machete it down, but if you grab it bare handed you get a nasty cut and any cut here gets infected like in half an hour, I am not really enjoy this patrol stuff, but, the panorama on top the hills takes yr breath away

Soldier Boy Dom

I think that was the only time I sign off like that. I

sound here like it is sort of summer camp, well I had not been in a fire fight yet. Either the next patrol or the one after that, ducking down, and earn my new nickname *Drizzle Britches* because the first time a tree next to me got peppered with rifle fire, I shit my pants. We were half way up some hill and the VC were on top, fire down at us; nobody got wounded or killed, but I had to go get in this stream and wash my pants and my nasty ass and we all got a big laugh out of it, not that I thought it funny then.

Sgt Richards, who was the patrol leader and forty-five-years old or so, give me a pep talk and told me first time he was in a big battle in Korea he shit his pants, too. I also knew, young as I was, they were keeping an eye on me to see if I would hold my mud.

A week or so later, we were coming down another hill and Sgt Ely give the fist, mean stop where you are, and we look over this rocky ridge, and there are about eight guys in green uniforms with those round hats, and before they even knew we were there we open up on them, and I know I hit two of em. The Nungs ran down and collect all the weapons and one of them was alive and not shot, so they tie him up and put this bamboo staff on his shoulders and gonna take him back to camp.

I come in camp and have to file an after action report on the teletype and do not say that I shot no one, but that we did KIA seven enemy and take one prisoner, and Maddy teases me and starts calling me Audie Murphy an shit, but I do know for sure I made my bones on that patrol, and I could feel the rest of the older guys were not gonna call me peach fuzz or diaper boy no more.

I know for sure we all put bullets in them, so I had not yet had any real reaction to killing someone. Some time later, when we were backing up another camp and some real hard-ass NVA types breech the wire, I know I smoked a few of them. I had a few very bad moments then, and I told Maddy I was gonna blow chunks. He said, "Fuck that Monk. It is us or them, buck up fuck ball, and notch yr carbine."

To this day, being there so early on, before any big units came and the war did become a WAR, I know in my soul had I been in any of those big battles I might not be here scrolling on down the page.

send me photographs and souvenirs

Butter

All really either scary or just terrible parts of that year, I have sort of suppressed. I choose to remember the funny or the insane stuff that is just part and parcel of war. One time, myself and bout six of us were flown by helicopter to Da Nang, a big old city and home to a giant US Air Force base. It was both to be a few days of r&r and also some training mission briefs, and a Net Control sync-up with Air Force pilots; they had both a very different protocol and style of radio communicating.

All well and good, on that part mostly boring, but a couple of day's along the Red River and eating at real restaurants, taking hot showers, and getting haircuts was still welcome. Some guys were again all about massage pallor or outright whore houses, but I had no interest in any of that; not being a prude, just having my own ideas about all that (clear to me now but was not then).

Anyway, big score. The Air Force has sort of a luxury supply and they live really well. So, getting ready to go back to Bong Son, I and an unnamed co-conspirator are on the tarmac, and see this two-ton truck unloading supplies into a big, metal building. Any Brooklyn boy knows good stuff falls off trucks. I might add here, the chopper crew chief was a guy I grew up with, name Billy

Mahoney.

In my finest light-bulb moment, I walk over and look at what is on and coming off that truck. Holy shit. Cases of beer, dry ice boxes marked perishable, and a couple bags of what is either onions or potatoes. Needless to go on, a few of the items wound up under a poncho liner right next to the helicopter we were gonna fly back on. It is what they called a *slick* ship, not with machine guns in both doors. Only three of us are going back that day, the other three are doing more operations and intel training. Plenty of room for my jackpot score.

Billy is laughing about *boy outta Brooklyn no Brooklyn outta da boy.* I tell him he can have one of the three cases of beer. No problem. We take off with a gun ship as escort, about halfway across the country. It is stunning looking down at the land and jungle. No one can, I think, really unless you see it, tell you how beautiful that land is.

We get back to camp, and Top is still in Da Nang, so, I bust open the one perishable box, and be still my heart, it is hi-price individually wrapped steaks. The two bags are indeed onion and potatoes, bout five pounds of each. Two full cases of San Miguel dark, and in the one small box I had grabbed is *butter!* Get the fuck outta here. Butter is like getting Michael Anthony to come give ya a million bucks. To say this stuff is not gonna keep is a big problem, but I get some big banana leaves and an empty foot locker. Ice is hard to get, but there is a small freezer for, of all things, medicine, so I wrap the steaks in leaves and put them on the bottom.

A week or so later, there is a nine-man patrol, the whole team. Me and the XO and one of the medics is alls left in camp. It is going to be three days out, in the back side of the biggest hill where there is some of the worst terrain and nasty jungle to hump through. My grand plan is to have a meal fit for kings ready when they get back.

I pulled out all the stops. I got this big board and put it on top of two empty mortar ammo boxes with a cut-up cammo parachute as a tablecloth. I did not get any Emily Post tableware or a matched set of plates and glasses, well that is just how it was. So, busy on the radio, I find out they are going to come back a day early. There was no contact and two of the guys were minor injured, one suffering really bad bug bites and the other a bad cut on his arm.

So, I do manage to get a bag of ice from the village, and an empty wash tub that I fill with bottles of beer. I set up a real Rube Goldberg BBQ deal out of a cut-in-half oil drum and some bamboo hunks twigs and all manner of burnable stuff. What I can tell you here is, when the guys got back to camp and could smell steak cooking, you could have swore it was Christmas Easter Fourth of July all at once. Not even bother to do anything but stack the weapons and send the Yards back to their part of the camp. It was glorious. Baked potatoes that I had done wrapped in banana leaf over the grill I made from a hunk of pierced steel plank. Butter, and I had fried up the onions with some Vietnamese veggies. All in all, it lifts my status with the team to exalted.

Only kink was when Top asked me where those steaks came from, and I just demure and tell him they were shipped from Okinawa, but did not tell him who they were shipped to.

It was about this same time when liberating other branches was sort of made a big deal, because some NCOs in Saigon had been arrested for stealing and selling stuff on the black market. We were in such a remote area, and I knew Top knew I had pulled some shit, but the meal was so good and we all had such a good time shooting the shit about home and about family and all like that, he never jam me about it.

There would come a time, a few months later, when a certain motorcycle was liberated but it became so hot and so close to a CID deal, that it just got back to where it was supposed to be, and safe to say, had it gotten away, I bet I would've gone to jail.

eight days a week

Dominic Albanese

Scared

Another letter:

There is big trouble, major uprising in some of the camps, and it is very bad, could get even worse, we are all on the move, to find out and either be part of or who knows, so much of this is so far over my head, and pay grade, I just gotta do what they tell me to, and I will write again soon

There are a few lines in that letter I choose not to share, because I was indeed really scared and sure sounded like a baby.

Dominic Albanese

Trouble

This would now all be about September 1964. As I had mentioned to Miss B, there was trouble, and it indeed was big enough trouble that it could have changed the course of the whole war. I know way more about it now than I did then. Then all I knew was radio chatter, from B team in Pleiku and from Ban Don and some other camps, that the Yards had a big case of the ass and were gonna shoot any Vietnamese soldiers they wanted to.

We were a split team of six guys and two non-airborne medics. In and out of Bong Son and Ban Don, up and down Route 14, by jeep or by foot. I knew a few of the NCOs and a couple of the officers, but only knew most of them by radio contact over the last few months.

How this all came to be was something that goes back in Vietnamese history to a long time ago. The Hmong Meo and tribes, known as Montagnard, or for short just Yards, were called moi by the Viets and that word means either savage or dirty depending on the tone. During the early liberations from Chinese overlords, both the Rade and Jarai tribes had been fierce fighters, but, as the more educated and more urban Viets got more power, most of the tribes were driven up in the hill country, where on both the Laos and Cambodian borders they had been for a long time anyhow. The major province of the hill country was called Daklak. On either side of the

Mekong River, there were lots of villages and haphazard farms, that grew tobacco, root plants, and raised ducks, pigs, and rice.

As early as 1960 or so, US Special Forces from Okinawa and Thailand had made camps and began to train what would come to be known as *Civilian Irregular Defense Groups* or, crazy as the Army is bout acronyms, CIDG. Unlike regular army units, the SF ones are small and live with whoever they are with as equals, and learn the traditions, culture and even some of them learn how to speak the local dialect. One more thing again I know now I did not know then, there were Yards, who were part French or part Vietnamese who had been indoctrinated to the Communist side and were active in fighting both the South and the Americans. Just not many of them and not part of the regular Peoples' Army; the ethnic distrust is very real. No matter that you can have a pretty smart group of Yards, they do not trust the Viets and the Viets do not trust them. Anything else so far I had seen, been in, or even knew of, was nowhere close to this eight day uprising that was, I will say it again, liable to upset the whole plan of cooperation and united forces against what we were told was communist aggressions.

A patrol out of one of the camps led by a guy I went through training with, SP-4 George Underwood, got hit hard and George got killed. He was the first guy I knew well to be killed, and it rocked me pretty hard. He was on the team with Lt Horn and Vinny Skebba, also both guys I knew well.

That team was sort of legendary. They were the guys that had smuggled a pair of Malaysian sun bears onto Okinawa and brought them into a local bar. That turned into a major MP SP AP mini-cop riot. They later would get their asses chewed big time by Captain Gillespie, a real hard ass, and his pal Major Brooks, another firm discipline guy. Any way, they then smuggle the two bears on a plane to Vietnam, and that almost got the Air Force pilot to turn around, but they did manage to get to Nha Trang, where the commanding officer of the 5th Group, then I think Col Spears, appropriated said bears, and one of them stayed in a pretty big cage behind HQ. I know for a fact when Col Francis Kelly went there, he kept the bear as a pet, too; they are about the size of a big dog, and not known at all for being mean or dangerous. I have no idea what happen to the other bear.

These guys are legends, they really are; Billy Snowhite, Marvin Compton (who, by the way, had a couple hundred pounds of Kentucky tobacco seeds sent to help the Yards grow better tobacco), Longmire (another guy who had Yorkshire pigs sent to mate with the smaller Vietnamese pigs to make more meat). It was an amazing time, and when the uprising happened, it stunned a lot of us, but there was this long-standing internal feud with anything to do with the LLDB – the Vietnamese special forces that the Yards just hated.

It got where a couple of the team captains and Major Brooks and Colonel Spears, all flew to Saigon to brief Generals Westmoreland and Maxwell Taylor. That part I do remember myself, because they came back with this utter asshole colonel who was some egghead guy who spoke college boy French and knew less about the Yards than anyone. What a shit show that was. I was sitting on an ammo box, watching him try to talk to about five of the Yard leaders, and they all look at him like he was from outer space. Cam, my Nung buddy, told Y Du that the colonel was speaking French, and all the Yards just cracked up. The colonel got all huffy and got back on the chopper and left.

There was this giant march set up from Bon Bring

back to Bon Su Par, and somehow the Special Forces officers managed to get the Yards to stand down and release the guys they had disarmed and locked up in the ammo bunker. Of course, the brass in Saigon was all about this absolutely shitty idea to mount *Operation Snatch*, that had it come to a big either ARVN or American unit coming in, very well could have led to some of us take sides with the Yards and shoot at our own guys.

That is not an exaggeration. It could have come to that. I was just about wore out from talking on the radio with the other camps, and HQ and giving the handset to a series of officers and way higher ranking NCOs to advise on the daily drama. Nobody got killed, no major battle went on. The saddest part of the whole thing, to me anyway, was the leader Y Don got cursed by the shaman and he went insane. We saw it happen, he got naked and ran into the bush, and he was never seen or heard from again.

I do also remember we had both Route 14 and Route 21 all ambush cover and would have let no trucks or tanks come down either road. That, like I've been saying, could have altered the course of the whole war.

I got really lucky after that. The commo guy in Gia Vuc had a family emergency and was sent home. We had another cross-train commo guy in Bong Son, so they sent me to Gia Vuc with Maddy, and we did our last part of '64 with the Civic Actions guys, cush duty, t-shirts, tooth brushes, comic books and bags of USA AID rice; jeep rides to all the outlying villages and give all the kids candy and presents, and yes, my first sexual contact with a Vietnamese.

She was about nineteen or so, and very pretty, very soft, and it just happened. I suspect she was hoping I would marry her and take her to America. I did speak to her about that, but even 56 years later, I feel like a dog for leading her on like that.

The next year, '65, I would meet a woman who worked at HQ, name Mai Li, and I did fall in love with her, but we never even kissed no less do boom boom. The Vietnamese word is *du*, and every story you ever hear about Saigon or Da Nang is bar girls and all that *I love you all night boom boom you buy me drink you give me money*. No money no honey, and like that. O man, what a jumble all this really is.

i see the harbor lights

Everybody's Listening

Of course I never wrote to Miss B bout any of that, but a letter in November near my birthday, from had to be Gia Vuc:

I am a year older, and very glad to be alive, given that 3 guys I know well or did are not. I am in a different place now doing Civic Action work, not combat patrols or like that, I am also now way better at the language, and can intone correctly, I have also learned most of the Rade dialect and can converse with them, but not as well. We will be going back to Head Quarters soon, and I have no idea what or where we are going next. I can't tell you bout the last month or so, I did tell you there was big trouble, but it was settle down, and not near as bad as it could have been. I am still very keen on the fact we are not supposed to tell much of what is really going on, just hi and how are you et cetera et cetera, very stupid, but I do know they take all this stuff very seriously I do not wanna get in trouble for say something I am not supposed to

as ever Dominic.

There is also now some big chatter about the Marines are coming and the 173rd Airborne and other big unit deployment. Mostly chatter, and when we do get to HQ, all the commo guys are called in to get the newest style hand-sets and we find out they have made all the radio stuff way more secure. Some patrols near Saigon found a fully operational VC radio set up where they were hearing a big percent of all our traffic.

Both Army and Navy, but not Air Force, we were told some air strike runs were known about before they happened, and the VC got outta there in a hurry. I have to say by this time I am not at all with the program, not at all, but I also hear Maddy tell me keep that shit to yourself do not say anything like that or they will gaffe you up and put you under the jail. There had been three I knew of guys who were indeed in big trouble, over disobeying an order or just tell some hi-rank to get fucked and eat shit an die. Common talk but not to an officer.

no such address no such zone

Buildup

Unable at this latter time to fully go back deep enough to the thinking and feeling of then, only a deep sorrow, and everything I thought was good, was true, was real, and was not. Brutal, I can say, filling sandbags, make busy work, and having my own ideas dealing with both the reality of obey make no waves, and do not say shit about feeling. Nobody gives a fuck bout any of that, and all the other guys are heavy drinkers, and, although they are hella crack troops, the weight of all this has its own effect.

Having pretty much built a new lifestyle camp for a nomadic brand of hill tribe people, there were some both funny and sad moments. Most of the Yards had their own way of cooking and keeping themselves fed. It was amazing to me; out on patrol with about fifty of them, they would stop in a clearing, gather up wood and any edible fruit or vines, and they all carry their own small black cook pots on back of the rucksacks we gave them. Rice was already so soaked from being in GI issue socks with herbs and water, they only had to heat it up. But some of them would go get a snake or a monkey or another quick kill, dress it, and cook it right over the open fire. We would argue with em sometimes about fires and smoke, and they would laugh at us, telling us they had been on these trails all their life, and were not gonna change how they operate. They were indeed very smart, but any abstract concept was impossible to translate or make them see it from our view.

By now, I can only look forward to going back to Okinawa. It is hot, summer is winter, and winter is summer here in Asia. I have a bad rash on my back and my hands are all crusty, keeping all the radio gear clean and in and out the web case. I got calluses and blisters on my feet and am for the most part just half ass jungle rot.

I can talk to Madison, we both love MAD magazine and do Don Martin bits, to the howling laughter of the Yards. It is now coming up on Christmas, 1964, and the word from HQ is, they are sending out a big holiday dinner. Thanksgiving had come and gone. I do recall that dinner they sent; it was not turkey but big hams and yams and apple pie. The Yards loved the pie, I do not think any of em had eaten apples before.

Something else, that all of a sudden, jumps back to me. The women were in charge. Yea there was a village or camp head man, but he had no say on a lot of things. The women own all the land, and the shaman does what they tell him to. I never did figure out some of the ritual stuff but knew this was the way it had been since the eighth or ninth century. There was not any of the ancestor worship or any of how the Vietnamese history really matter to any of the Hmong Meo or Tribes. They had a now is all that counts attitude about it all. New Year's does not come till February for them.

By January '65, I get pulled back to HQ, and the next assignment for me is Pli Ma So, about fifteen miles outside Nha Trang, and not a big camp at all, but a way station for Communications with a full Quonset hut, full of big sets and teletype machines, with this giant generator to power it all up. I stayed there for a month, learning as I went, then training new O5B guys on newer handsets and way better battery packs, so ya did not have to carry the hand crank power unit. There are also these new antenna sets that are round not poles and have this really neat thing like a spring launch deal, to get up and target the next telemetry area.

I miss the guys back on my team, and really here am only with some CIA guys and the in and out of new fresh meat fed to the now getting bigger and bigger by the month. I leave there and do get told I can take three-week r&r, in either Hong Kong or Australia. I tell Sgt Major, I would rather just go back to Okinawa. He has a lot of paperwork stuff he needs some help with, and I tell him I am a good typist and I will help him all I can.

I might mention here Sergeant Majors are as close to God as it gets in the Army. I had a very close relation to that one Sgt Major Edge. He, like a lot of them, already had twenty years in, and could retire any time they wanted; most all of them stay for thirty because it is the highest enlisted rank, and they retire at about the same pay rate as a Captain.

1965 sees a major upswing in troops, both Special Forces and conventional ones. The Navy now has three carriers just offshore, and the Air Force is doing major bombing runs up and down the Laos and Vietnam border. I hear the chatter from Kham Duc and Do Sai, up round the North South line, and they are saying some of it feels like earthquakes.

feel so broke up i wanna go home

Fictions

Enough about war, danger, fear, all the trouble and angst of my now lost youth. More about Miss B, the letters, and the reason all this is being put to a book.

Almost a proclamation to all teachers, who might or might not know how much they affect someone early in this whole deal called life. Why did I choose to write it seems only to her, and detail, try to explain, and yes, try to learn how to write better, and almost make her proud of me? I bet somewhere there are some big studies done about who and how influences mentors teachers parents siblings peers, all that. Make a person either grow, or stay stunted in some age bracket, where feeling safe is way more of import than taking risks, allowing one's self to fly, bounce, land and get up then keep going.

Letter dated March '65:

> *I am going back to Okinawa, and with just some good moves, I can stay there, or come back to CONUS, and be, outta all this madness. I will tell you the whole mood has changed here, more guys getting killed, and way more ambushes, outright camp overruns, and this is now, really starting to look like a war. I am, not in any trouble, but with 18 months in that equal 3 full tours, I am eligible to rotate out. I do not have my orders yet but will go to HQ sometime this or next week, and a few*

*others of us are due to leave too. I have no idea
what is next, but I have a bit less than a full year
left, and they already give me these speeches, bout
re-enlist, and make a career out of the Army. I
think I would rather go blind deaf and dumb than
stay in the Army*

I did now know some things that deep trouble me,
mostly about some after action reports I file, and they
come back printed, in almost exact opposite. I ask Top
about some of the what-seems-like fiction, and he told
me, not mad but serious, "Do not bother me bout any of
that, and just keep yr dumb ass alive so I do not have to
deal wit your mother."

I know he had been to HQ on the phone back to the
USA to comfort, or at least offer condolence, for a guy
he grew up with and they had been in the Army together
for more than twenty years.

Another thing that was happening is the Sea Bees,
and some private contractor companies, were building
way bigger way more secure and better equipped camps.
They had started MIKE force, and Special Operations
Groups, plus some CIA shit, outta Laos and now here,
with unmarked choppers, and no badge or patch
uniforms, and there were now some Rangers, from Fort
Lewis and Fort Benning, doing search and kill missions.

O man, I am dreaming about the beach on Okinawa
and the easy duty I hope to get. This time frame is
cloudy at best. Because my feet were so infected and
crusty, it was pretty sure I was not going on more
patrols. I think there are two more letters here, then,
that I am not gonna quote from, cause I do just go on
about how bad I feel and how I wanna go home. Not
anything you're supposed to be talking about. All that
gung ho rah rah hoop de doo that I have lost any taste or

idea about.

I did get to go to Nha Trang and stay there for most of March and ten days in April, and I flew back to Okinawa with some field grade officers and some I bet CIA guys; but I sat there in that web seat, only hoping my feet would get healed up, and I did leave all my good stuff with Ely and Maddy.

My Dear Miss B

I had never a thought romantic about Miss B. She was to me the rock the web the wonder of somebody who I knew cared and would always answer my letters. There seem to be some missing from the whole set I got, because there are only four letters from Okinawa, the last one dated July '65, and I did not leave there till March of '66. I can't help but wonder what I would have said.

Of all the guys I was in the Army with, Madison was the only one I stayed in touch with, and met up with back in the USA, and we stayed very close right up till he died; in fact I spoke to him about four hours before he died. 2004 I think.

I think this might just be a good time to end this story, book, memoir, memorial, tribute or whatever a reader wants to call it, to enjoy, trip on, or have an associated timeline of their life, in the timeline of mine.

Dominic Albanese

endpaper

I just read this long psychological paper on how you are not at over-70 who you were at 14. All this was indeed a labor of love. Jagged capsule memories, with almost some kind of cinéma vérité of places faces people and events; I am in Kaiser Park, walking, and can be there now in my mind. I am going up the stairs at Mark Twain, and meeting Miss B the first few times, and knowing this was a major point for me, then and now. How is that possible? You know what? I do not know.

Validation, acceptance, terms that in 1959 were not even a part of any language I spoke then. That small leather-bound copy of Emily Dickinson's poems is farfetched? I think not. Transistor radio songs, lines from them haunt me still. As does that whole time of innocence. Nobody can ever take that from me. I only wish I did remember it a bit more lucidly.

I will not go on here about post-Vietnam; that story is so over told anyhow. I will say I have spent fifty years of study and reading to try to understand the history, culture and depth of that land. I have been back there three times, once in fact as a visiting poet with some Canadians and Australians. We all read, and my Vietnamese accent was a great source of enjoyment. The English students there pointed out to me some rather embarrassing tonal mistakes.

I am not a professional veteran, or some rah rah guy who revels in all that, and I never have been. There are a whole lot of people post-1966 who never even knew I was in the Army, no less in Vietnam. In fact, a very dear friend of mine from back then just told me, she had never heard any of that from me.

Why does anybody write? In publishing twelve books of poems so far, I have no factual or intellectual explanation to give. I know it was Miss B who, even though I already loved to read, made me understand and care about what language and words are really all about. I will bet you I will struggle to grasp all about that long as I get days above ground, to work think write and live.

This also being my first book of not poetry, it is leading me to the next one - *101 Elsie Street*. San Francisco 1967-87, and, like I said at the beginning of this one: *a lot has happened.*

I fear here to mention some and somehow leave out others, because my support network is wide and means more to me than just a shout out or tip o the hat can say. Kris at Poetic Justice Books and Arts gets all the credit for how this looks and cleaning up my babble style. Judith Jones gets a big hug and kiss, for adding things telling me things from her *JJFROMDABLOCK* perspective and helping Kris with cleanup duty. My Facebook friends, almost all of em, have been a big help. Seb Doubinsky, Christina Quinn, Steven Gillis, Declan Conlon, Carter Monroe, Susan Andrews, Karen Miller, Roni Hoffman, Corina Pelloni ... my sister-in-law Carol, too ... all y'all, give me support, ideas and comments that made me want to finish this and make it the best I was able to.

And finally in memorial to Spain, Maddy, Tommy, Bobby, my parents, my other now gone to rest deep friends, I pass em all here, as I thank em and love em as they have loved me.

about the author

Dominic Albanese lives, writes and fishes on Florida's Treasure Coast.

colophon

Dear Miss B, by Dominic Albanese,
was set with SITKA, *alfresco* and COURIER NEW fonts
by SpiNDec, Port Saint Lucie, Florida
The jacket and covers were designed by
Kris Haggblom, Treasure Coast, Florida